The Usual Error

The Usual Error

Why We Don't Understand Each Other
And 34 Ways to Make It Better

First Edition

Pace and Kyeli Smith

illustrated by Martin Whitmore

CONNECTION PARADIGM PRESS
AUSTIN, TEXAS

First Edition
Last revised December 21, 2008

Book design by Megan Elizabeth Morris (www.virtualmagpie.com)
Cover by Martin Whitmore (www.martinwhitmore.com) and
Megan Elizabeth Morris (www.virtualmagpie.com)

ISBN: 978-0-9821621-0-1
Library of Congress Control Number: 2008910953
Published by Connection Paradigm Press
(www.connectionparadigm.net)

For feedback, inquiries related to the book, or for consulting, speaking, and workshop inquiries, email paceandkyeli@usualerror.com.

For more information about interpersonal communication, including an electronic copy of this book in HTML and PDF form, visit www.usualerror.com.

for Dru

CONTENTS

Acknowledgments . . . . p. iv

Welcome! . . . . p. 1

Part I: Communication Dynamics

1: The usual error . . . . p. 5

2: Different communication styles . . . . p. 10

3: Different personality types . . . . p. 14

4: The other half of communication . . . . p. 17

5: Checking in . . . . p. 22

6: I already know this,
but I need to hear you say it again . . . . p. 28

7: What problem are you trying to solve? . . . . p. 32

8: Feeling considered . . . . p. 36

Part II: Boundaries

9: Holding healthy boundaries . . . . p. 42

10: Fierceness . . . . p. 47

i

Contents

11: Ask for what you need . . . . p. 52

12: I am not green . . . . p. 57

13: "I" statements . . . . p. 61

14: It's not all about me . . . . p. 66

Part III: Turning Conflict into Communication

15: What did you intend? . . . . p. 74

16: The next time I ask for $1000,
just give me a veggie burger instead! . . . . p. 79

17: We're on the same team . . . . p. 84

18: Coming to terms . . . . p. 88

19: Meta-communication . . . . p. 95

20: Memory . . . . p. 99

21: Trust your future self . . . . p. 105

22: Giving permission to disappoint . . . . p. 108

Part IV: Conflict Resolution

23: The only way out is through . . . . p. 114

24: The William James zone . . . . p. 118

25: The lollipop . . . . p. 124

26: What do I get out of being right? . . . . p. 133

27: Reflection . . . . p. 139

28: Verbal aikido . . . . p. 143

Contents

Part V: Positivity!

29: "That makes me really happy!" . . . . p. 154

30: It's okay to have problems . . . . p. 157

31: Knowing is half the battle . . . . p. 161

32: Rephrasing things positively . . . . p. 165

33: Teasing . . . . p. 174

34: Endings . . . . p. 181

Stories and Examples . . . . p. 186

Illustrations . . . . p. 190

Acknowledgments

The Usual Error was conceived and written with the help of many people. We offer our thanks to the following people for their contributions:

Our first fans: We began this journey in April of 2006 by giving a communication presentation to an audience of 25, only a few of whom were familiar faces. Afterwards, nearly all of you made time to tell us how life-changing our presentation had been. Without your support and encouragement, we would have never gotten any further than that one presentation.

Alanis Morissette: *(The only way out is through)* You have been an inspiration and a guiding light in Kyeli's life since she was just a lonely kid. Your lyrics have sung right into her heart and kept her going through some of the darkest times in her life. We offer our deepest gratitude, and are honored to share in the fixing of the world with you.

Breanna Bell: For all of the talking and listening.

Heather Renwick: You've been one of our biggest fans from the beginning. The glee with which you implement our ideas brings joy to us as well!

Judy Davidson and Tony Lorino: For your love and support, and for caring for Dru while we wrote and edited the book.

Acknowledgments

Kit O'Connell and Reesa Brown: *(Ask for what you need & Coming to terms)* Not just for your specific topics, but also for your endless patience and willingness to listen and help.

Mary Hoelscher: For your support and encouragement from the beginning.

Megan Elizabeth Morris: Your boundless enthusiasm and support keeps us going. Your work makes our work far more enjoyable, not to mention possible. You're like the secret power behind the throne!

Michael Faires-McClellan: *(It's not all about me)* In one discussion among many, you mentioned this. It clicked with us, and we realized its importance. Your friendship and support has helped us grow and learn about communication and ourselves.

Pam McElhinney: *(I am not green)* You took the time to listen and explain, and managed to reword a difficult concept so we could better understand it and better explain it to others. We wouldn't have gotten this far without your help.

Robert C. Kahlert: *(What problem are you trying to solve?)* Your frequent asking of this question in a software engineering context led us to ask it in other contexts as well. It's been very useful; thank you.

Robie Kentspeth: *(Coming to terms & What did you intend?)* With us from the start, you and your family have been supportive and helpful. We deeply appreciate all you've done for us.

Sera Smith: You helped us with the first draft of the book, and you helped us learn, practice, and master all the communication techniques we now teach. Thank you.

Kira April Parra, Kelan Wieloch, Amanda Braman-Ray, Judy Davidson, Tanya Martin-McClellan, Vicki Borah Bloom, Oliver Danni Green, Michael Faires-McClellan, Brieann "Cricket" Chapple, Jon Curtis, Green Adams-Hanley, Tony Lorino, Dusty Lorino, Beth Lorino, and Paula Duckhorn: For editing and proofreading. Your suggestions helped immensely!

Acknowledgments

We would also like to thank all of our friends and co-creators from the Reclaiming tradition. We learned about *checking in* and many other amazing communication techniques from you!

Last, but certainly not least, to all the people who come to our workshops: thank you for listening, offering feedback and constructive criticism, and for encouraging us to keep going. We wouldn't be here without you, and we are very grateful!

WELCOME!

Everything in this book, each chapter and each concept, is something we (Pace and Kyeli) have used to communicate with each other and with loved ones, friends, family, coworkers, and sometimes even strangers. We're telling you the stories of our lives, though some of the names and details have been changed. In our time together, we have talked, fought, talked, cried, talked, yelled, talked, argued, and talked. We've learned enormous amounts about ourselves, each other, and the world around us, and we'd like to share what we've learned with you.

Be honest.

Honesty is the unspoken assumption behind every chapter in this book. In order for these techniques to work for you, you must be honest with yourself and with others. Tell the truth, the whole truth, and nothing but the truth. These communication tools are powerful, and like any powerful tool, they can be misused. If you are honest, you will use them well.

Practice and teach.

Think of this as a workbook rather than an instruction manual. All of the chapters tie together with each other, so you may want to read it twice. You'll also get a lot more out of it if you *practice*. As you read each chapter, think about how the topic has come up in your life, how it could improve your life, and how you could explain the concepts to your partner. (Throughout the book, we use "partner" to refer to either your romantic partner or, more generally, your communication partner. This could be your business partner, coworker, friend, family member, or anyone else with whom you communicate.) If you read with the aim of teaching, your understanding deepens.[1] Even better, share this book with your partner and talk about each chapter as you read it together. The best way for you to become a better communicator is to communicate!

A wise man learns by the mistakes of others, a fool by his own.
— Latin Proverb

This book is the fruit of our folly.
May it bring you wisdom!

---

1   We learned this by reading *The 7 Habits of Highly Effective People* by Stephen Covey.

PART I:
COMMUNICATION
DYNAMICS

Chapter I:

The usual error

The usual error is assuming that other people are just like you.

Assuming that others think like you, would react to a certain situation like you would, or value the same things you do — all of these are examples of the usual error. Psychologists call it *projection bias:* we project our own perceptions, opinions, and emotions onto another person, as if our experiences were theirs. We all do this. We do it *all the time;* that's why it's called the *usual* error. Making the usual error isn't something to fear, it's something to notice. In our experience, most miscommunications stem from the usual error. When you learn to recognize that it's happening, you can turn arguments into opportunities for understanding.

The usual error manifests in many forms, often subtly. We assume that others' boundaries are the same as ours. We assume that others' communication styles and personality types are the same as ours. We assume that others can know what we're thinking and know what we need without us having to ask. We assume that others' definitions for words are the same as ours and we judge the intent behind their words based on our own assumptions. We assume that others' memories of shared events are the same as ours. We assume that others value the same things we do and fear the same things we do. We assume that others' bodies have the same physical limitations and thresholds as ours. We assume all kinds of things about other people *all the time.*

Everyone does this. It's not bad or wrong; it's part of being human. The usual error is something that happens behind the scenes, in the subconscious mind. We've even made the usual error in this book! We teach communication techniques that work well for us, but they might not all work as well for you.

Kyeli's Story: Making the Usual Error

Pace runs her fingers through my hair. Her fingers tangle, rub my scalp. I pull away slightly, "Don't rat my hair!" Pace made the usual error — what she was doing feels good to her when I do the same thing, but it doesn't feel good to me.

I cook up some Bagel Bites for Pace. I give them to her and notice the slight crinkle in her nose. I ask her if there's a problem. "Yeah," she says, "these are... um... too done for me." I made the usual error — I like my Bagel Bites to be ridiculously brown and she likes hers still squishy.

I finish using the internet and close the browser window. Pace sits down and grumbles at me, "Why do you close the window?" I made the usual error — I like to close all the windows when I'm done at the computer, but Pace prefers to leave them open.

It's 11pm. I call my mom, and am surprised when she groggily answers the phone. "Were you asleep? I'm sorry!" I made the usual error — I stay up late, so 11pm isn't late to me, but to my mom, it's after bedtime!

Katie asks me for assistance in dyeing her hair. I wind up pulling her hair a lot, and hurting her scalp — again, I made the usual error. You have to pull pretty hard on my hair to hurt me, so I assumed

Katie's scalp was as tough as mine, but hers is actually quite sensitive.

Laura is visiting and we're all watching a movie. Pace and I talk to each other and at the characters. Laura gets annoyed, because she prefers silence during movies. Another case of the usual error — we were engaging in our typical behavior, assuming she wouldn't mind because we don't!

Rachel scoops up my kitten and ruffles the fur on his belly. The kitten gives her a deep scratch. She made the usual error — her cat loves that sort of affection, so she didn't think about my kitten not wanting the same treatment.

Pace gets up from the couch in the middle of an episode of *Angel* and I hit the pause button. "Don't pause it!" she shouts. I had forgotten she dislikes interruptions in the middle of a show and since I don't mind them, I paused. The usual error again!

The usual error boils down to assuming that others experience the exact same reality we do. Since our own perspective is the only one we experience directly, we make these kinds of assumptions a lot. These guesses and projections about other people allow us to get by, but unfortunately, most of the time our assumptions are wrong. When someone doesn't act as we expect, we often react with surprise or anger. The other person's behavior violates our expectations of a nicely ordered and predictable world. Because they do things that we wouldn't, we think that makes them wrong.

That's one way to look at it, but another way is to appreciate the differences between yourself and others. It can be hard to remember this when you're feeling angry, afraid, or upset, but think about this: how boring would it be if everyone were the same? It's the differences between us that allow for admiration, cooperation, learning, synergy, and in many cases, love. You have the power; you can choose to appreciate these differences instead of getting angry about them. Keep that in mind when you notice yourself making the usual error.

The usual error can even be helpful! It's a way that people subconsciously communicate their needs. For example, if a friend or lover is giving you a back massage, they will probably rub you the way *they* would like to be rubbed. They're making the usual error and you can use it to your advantage, or at least to *their* advantage. Take note of what they do, how they massage, and what spots they focus on. Then when you rub their back, you'll have a good idea of what will feel good to them. This technique also works for sex, if you account for anatomical differences.

You may notice a similarity between the usual error and the Golden Rule: "Do unto others as you would have them do unto you." However, others may not want or need the same things as you. *The usual error is the flaw in the Golden Rule.*

Joan and Larry's Example:
The Flaw in the Golden Rule

Joan is honest, open, and blunt. She appreciates when her friends "call her on her shit" and respects those who don't "sugar-coat the truth."

Larry is sensitive, emotional, and kind. He appreciates when his friends offer help in a gentle way and respects those who are considerate of others' feelings.

If Joan acted according to the Golden Rule, she would do unto Larry as she would have Larry do unto her. She would prefer that Larry be open and blunt with her, and so according to the Golden Rule, she will treat Larry openly and bluntly as well. This will not be a kindness to Larry, who will be hurt by Joan because he will find her harsh and disrespectful. Communication won't happen.

Likewise, if Larry acted according to the Golden Rule, he would treat Joan gently, being careful not to offend her. This would not be a kindness to Joan, who will not listen to Larry because she will consider him wishy-washy and spineless. Communication won't happen.

The Golden Rule makes the usual error; it assumes that other people are just like you. "Of course others wish to be treated exactly like I wish to be treated!" How about instead, "Do unto others as they would have you do unto them"? This is the *Platinum Rule*. It's the version of the Golden Rule that doesn't make the usual error.

Noticing and correcting ourselves when we make the usual error has improved our lives in many ways. We see others more clearly, no longer merely seeing mirror images of our own faces. We appreciate other people's differences and strengths. When we poke our heads out from our bubble of assumptions, we hear the truth spoken by our loved ones. We still make the usual error all the time, but now that we're more aware of it, we can correct it. We now communicate with others in a way that is clearer, more true, and more free from the assumptions that blind us. As we continue, we'll show you how we correct various forms of the usual error in our daily lives, and how you can do it too!

Chapter 2:

Different communication styles

We all look at the world through special glasses created by us, for us. Kyeli sees the world through Kyeli-colored glasses and Pace sees the world through Pace-colored glasses. Your mom, your best friend, the mailman, the Dalai Lama, Alanis Morissette, and you each have your own lenses to see the world through. No matter how close we get to our loved ones, we can never see the world in exactly the same way they do. This lends itself not only to the usual error, but also to *different communication styles*. Everyone communicates in their own way. We all have our own idiosyncrasies, phrases, definitions, meanings, and understandings that belong to us and us alone. We each have our own issues and emotional baggage as well as our own unique ways of interpreting what we hear.

Kyeli's Story: Differences in Our Household

In our home, there are three people (not counting the cats) and each of us has a different way of communicating, both verbally and non-verbally.

Pace tends to process things logically and often thinks out loud. It's common for her to stop mid-sentence and change her opinion because she's talked herself out of something. She's also learning to make her body language more clearly reflect her internal emotions. She didn't emote much growing up, so it's still challenging for her.

I tend to repeat myself in different ways. Our canonical example of this comes from my days as a preschool teacher: "The block center is closed for the rest of the day. No more playing with the blocks. We'll be doing things outside of the block center this afternoon." I also speak in stories. I emote strongly and clearly, so it's often easy to tell what I'm feeling, and it's very difficult for me to hide my emotions (not that I usually want to).

Dru is still developing his communication style, and often has to start over and mutter a lot before his thoughts are coherent enough to share with us.

These differences inspired many of the chapters in this book. It's a constant delight to learn how to better communicate with each other.

These differences aren't bad. Often we become frustrated when others don't communicate in a way we can easily understand. We feel like their communication style is *wrong* because it is not like ours. That's one perspective, but remember that you can choose to change your perspective; you can appreciate others' differences in communication styles as part of what makes them different, unique, and beautiful.

One way to better understand someone's communication style is to have dinner with their family. Typically, children learn their communication style from their families of origin, and it takes effort to change it as an adult. Seeing how a person's family interacts can yield great insights into how they learned to communicate the way they do.

Kyeli's Story: "I'm Not Yelling!"

One night, we were having a conversation and I got excited. I was being really loud when suddenly I noticed that Pace was cowering. I stopped mid-sentence to ask what was the matter and she eeked out, "You're *yelling!* You must be really upset!"

"Oh, no!" I responded, "I'm not yell... okay, I'm yelling, but I'm not upset, just... loud!"

My family is largely Irish/Italian. Family events at my grandmother's house were loud and unruly, with adults having excited, animated conversations at various tables and kids running through the house and slamming doors. My dad gets loud when he gets excited, and as a result, I do too. I also took more than 8 years of choir and theater, so I have no problems being heard. I tend to be loud and get louder when emotional.

Pace's background is very different from mine. In her house, raised voices meant someone was *angry*.

Once we established that Pace was making the usual error, we boiled it down to a major difference in how we each communicate. Now, whenever I hear myself getting loud I remind her, "I'm not angry! Just loud!"

Learning how you communicate will not only help you, but will also help those with whom you communicate.

Pace's Story: "I'm Really Okay"

I know I have difficulty emoting, so if Kyeli seems to be misunderstanding me, I'll pause the conversation to double-check with her. I'll say something like, "Perhaps I seem to be upset, but I'm not. I'm actually okay."

That's often enough for Kyeli to feel sufficiently reassured to continue a conversation. It helps that she knows me well enough to know what's going on when this happens; we've learned that emoting is one big difference in our communication styles, and we find ways around or through it so that we can still successfully communicate.

The better we get to know someone, the more likely we are to fall into the myth that our partner sees the world as we do. Keeping in mind that we *don't* see the world in the same way, no matter how close we get, will help us get along more smoothly and enable us to communicate more clearly. When we see and embrace our differences, we remember that it's wonderful and beautiful to be who we are, no matter how we are.

CHAPTER 3:

DIFFERENT PERSONALITY TYPES

People have *different personality types.* This will cause differences in communication styles, but also causes more fundamental differences in what people want and how people think. It's no surprise that if people see the world in different ways, they will communicate about it in different ways.

Personality tests are fun and informative when used to explore different personality types. Are you an ENFP? A Random Gentle Love Master? An Enneatype 7?[1] There are hundreds

---

1   ENFP is from the Myers-Briggs test (www.myersbriggs.org), Random Gentle Love Master is from the OKCupid Dating Persona Test (www.okcu-

of personality tests out there; have some fun taking them with your partners and friends and discuss your results. These tests are often either eerily accurate or extremely off the mark; either way, they can provide good insight into the personalities of those with whom you interact on a regular basis.

Pace's Story:

It Might Be Nice to See a Movie on Sunday

I'm a P on the Myers-Briggs test.[2] I'm so P I always score almost entirely P and very little J (the opposite of P). P stands for "Perceiving" and J stands for "Judging," as in analyzing. P people see the world as a sea of possibilities and are often said to have their heads in the clouds. J people deal with reality instead of possibility and are often said to have their feet on the ground. P people like to have things open and flexible, whereas J people like to have things settled and decided.

My ex-girlfriend Tessa is a J. This caused many communication problems for us. In one of our phone conversations, I said, "It might be nice to see a movie on Sunday." She heard, "We now have plans to see a movie on Sunday at 2:00." I forgot about it, since in my perception we hadn't finalized any plans. When I heard a knock at the door on Sunday at 2:00 I was surprised and confused. I wondered who it could be, since I wasn't expecting anyone. Lo and behold, it was Tessa! She was ready to go and upset to find me still unshowered and in my pajamas. Mayhem ensued.

---

pid.com), and Enneatype 7 is from the Enneagram Personality Type Indicator (www.enneagraminstitute.com).

2   A good book on Myers-Briggs personality types is *Please Understand Me, An Essay on Temperament Styles*, by David Keirsey and Marilyn Bates.

When we first talked about possible movie plans, I was talking about flexible possibilities, but she was hearing settled realities. In a conversation, each person filters things through their own personal worldview. What one person intends may be very different from what the other person hears.

After Tessa and I figured out what had happened, we learned to make allowances for each other. She tried to remember that sometimes I talk in hypotheticals and I tried to remember that she's more comfortable dealing with decided plans than with a slew of possibilities.

To help avoid this communication problem in the future, I added more qualifiers when talking about ideas rather than actualities: "It would maybe possibly be nice to see a movie on Sunday, or perhaps some other time instead." These additional possibility words helped Tessa realize that I was speaking hypothetically, whereas a single possibility word might have been silently gobbled up by her J-filter.

Another thing that can be fun to do with personality tests is to read summaries of the strengths and weaknesses of each personality type. Pay particular attention to the strengths of personality types that differ from yours. If you can see the good side of a personality trait that has vexed you in the past, your interactions with everyone who has that personality trait will improve because you'll be interacting with them out of respect and understanding rather than annoyance.

Everyone has a unique personality. Even two people with the same personality type will have different likes, dislikes, issues, feelings, emotions, and lives. Awareness of these amazing differences bolsters our communication and makes us kinder and more compassionate. Also, appreciating people's differences helps us avoid the usual error!

Chapter 4:

The Other Half of Communication

When people communicate, they usually want one of two things: to solve a problem or to be heard. The stereotype is that men want to problem solve and women want to be heard, but regardless of stereotypes, being truly heard is a rare and precious gift. Most of the other chapters of this book talk about talking, but listening is *the other half of communication*.

Simply having someone — anyone — to listen to you can be immensely valuable. A straightforward example of this is the "cardboard cutout dog" effect.[1]

Pace's Story: Cardboard Cutout Keith

After spending a frustrating hour trying to fix a computer program I'm writing, I finally resort to asking my coworker Keith for help.

Keith: Okay, what's the problem?

Me: Addition isn't working.

Keith: How so?

Me: Well, I've got these two numbers, here and here, and my program is supposed to add them, but it's giving me the wrong answer.

Keith: Okay...

Me: So, these numbers come from this other program over here... Oh. The other program spits out text, not a number. You can't add text and a number. That's the problem. Thanks for your help, Keith.

Keith: No problem!

Sometimes we get lost in the trees and can't see the forest. In this example, Pace's focus on adding the two numbers made her lose sight of the larger issue of where the numbers were coming from. The act of explaining the problem in its full context forced her to take a step back and see the bigger picture, which helped her find and fix the problem.

---

[1]   We read the "cardboard cutout dog" story at www.sjbaker.org/humor/cardboard_dog.html. Don't worry, we'll explain what it means after the story.

Eventually, so the legend goes, someone thought of the clever idea of saving money by buying a cardboard cutout dog for the office and letting people explain things to the dog, rather than taking up the time of highly paid software engineers or boring the receptionist with technical jargon.

The cardboard cutout dog effect works because the act of thoroughly explaining a problem to someone requires that we take the time to precisely re-examine all of our circumstances, actions, assumptions, and choices, and the reasons behind them. We have to think the problem through from the ground up. When we come to the problem fresh like this, we see the incorrect reasoning or subtle errors that we missed before.

If listening is this powerful even when the listener is made of cardboard, imagine how powerful it can be with two fully engaged humans! Being truly, honestly heard without judgment or interruption creates a feeling of safety and acceptance, allowing us to converse with ourselves on a deeper emotional level, opening up and dealing with things that we might never touch otherwise.

Walter's Example:

A Conversation with Yohn[2]

"Can I talk to you for a minute, Yohn?" said Walter.

"..." said Yohn.

"It's just that I'm so pissed off about the whole thing, you know? I mean, what right has he got?!"

"..." said Yohn.

---

2   This conversation took place between two characters in the video game *Suikoden Tactics*. It was actually Kyril who had that conversation with Yohn, but the name Kyril looked so much like "Kyeli" that we changed it to avoid confusion.

"Um, well, yeah, I guess I would be pretty angry if I were in his shoes. But that doesn't make it okay. I mean, I have to do this, and I can't do it with him in my way!"

"..." said Yohn.

"Yeah, I guess you're right, Yohn. That's a lame excuse. I don't *have* to do this at all. I guess I'm just blaming him because... because I'm afraid."

"..." said Yohn.

"Thanks, Yohn. Talking with you has helped me a lot."

"..." said Yohn, and smiled.

Helping someone else feel heard takes a willingness to listen to someone and care about what they say. You might judge what the other person is saying, you might have a strong opinion about it, or you might have some advice you feel will help. Let it all go for now, keep your attention on their words, and accept their experience as it is.

Kyeli's Story: Falling in Love

Sera and I were downstairs in the kitchen, talking. She hit a nerve: a topic that made my heart race and fear well up in me, so I said, "Whoa, I need to think deeply about this; this feels important and big." I started talking about my self-image and my struggles with self-esteem.

I talked and talked. Sera listened in silence. I cried. I thought. I dug. I unearthed. I talked. I rambled. I kept asking, "Why am I even talking about this?" Sera listened in silence.

After about an hour, sitting on the couch, leaning on Sera, deep in thought, I flippantly muttered, "You know, if I ever met anyone *exactly* like me, I would totally fall in love with her."

The universe paused, waited for me to realize what I'd said. Sera remained silent.

I burst into tears, realizing that I had just fallen in love with myself.

I couldn't have gotten to that realization at that time without Sera's patience and quiet listening. If she had said, "Do you realize what you just said?" instead of waiting for me to get there myself, it wouldn't have felt as intense to me, because it had to come from *me*. This is an example I often remember when I think about the power of listening.

The power of truly listening sparks revelations, eases fear and pain, and helps find and solve mistakes. It can change your life as well as the lives of others.

Chapter 5:

Checking In

In this hectic world, we often feel like no one truly listens to us. Our listeners rarely give us careful, full attention. No one teaches us to listen deeply, and it's not something we know to practice on our own. *Checking in* allows us to experience the power of listening and truly being heard.[1]

Here's how checking in works. You sit down in a circle with one or more others. A rough circle is fine, as long as everyone

---

1   We learned this from the Reclaiming tradition of neopaganism, who in turn learned it from a practice in group therapy and consensus process.

can see and hear everyone else. Someone chooses to begin and starts talking. While it's their turn to talk, it's your turn to listen. All you need to do is *listen*. When you feel the urge to speak, reply, argue, or help, let it go. This is not the time for that; this is the time to listen. Avoid little acknowledgment noises like "Mm-hmm," or "Yeah." Those are appropriate for a conversation, but checking in is something different. Silence makes it much easier to listen.

Inner silence is important, too. Listen with your full attention. Try not to get distracted or anxious about what you're going to say when it's your turn. There's no need to plan ahead; it's much more powerful and effective if your words come from your heart in the now. When it's your turn, you won't be making a speech or trying to impress anyone.

While it's your turn to listen, focus 100% of your attention on the speaker. Look into the speaker's eyes. Hear the words they say. Feel the emotions they express. Share the experience of their life as they communicate with you. You know you're being a good listener when you have no attention to spare for judging, coming up with a reply, or thinking about what you'll say on your turn. Offer them the gift of truly being heard, and in turn they will offer this gift to you as well.

Nonverbal feedback while listening is fine as long as it's not distracting to the speaker. Our favorite way to give nonverbal feedback is called "twinkling." Twinkling is a gesture made by wiggling the fingers of both hands, like you're playing random notes on a piano but with your fingers fully outstretched. It communicates "I agree," or "I feel that way too." Twinkling is a good way to let the speaker know that you are sharing or relating to their experience without verbally interrupting their flow. If twinkling feels unnatural or uncomfortable to you, you can simply nod in agreement.

When it's your turn to check in, you can talk about whatever thoughts or emotions happen to pass through you at that moment. You can talk about the events of your day, you can let off steam about things that are **bothering** you, or you can just be silent for a little while. No one **will interrupt** you. No one will argue with you or tell you you're **not allowed** to think or feel that way. No one will jump in to give **you** advice or to tell you about a time they felt like that too. Everyone will simply listen to you with their full attention. When you're finished, say "check," and then it's the next person's turn. Each person in the circle gets a chance to check in.

Kevin's Example: Triad Check-In Time

Kevin and his partners Molly and Heather are sitting together on the couch. It's been a long day, and he's feeling grateful for this time of relaxing and unwinding. When Molly asks for a check-in, he initially feels a rush of stage fright and fear of what might surface, but he reminds himself that he will only say what he wants to say. He can even simply say "check" if he wants to say nothing, with no repercussion. This positive, voluntary view of things calms his nerves, and he nods.

Molly goes first. She talks about her day, the frustrations of her job, some of the deeper thoughts she's been pondering, and a few delightful random things that happened to be on her mind, like the particularly sharp flavor of the cheese she ate at lunch and a plot twist in a book she read two years ago. Kevin and Heather listen. They hear her words, the tone of her voice, how it conveys her energy level and her emotions. They see the enthusiasm in her face and her posture as she speaks of a new project at work that excites her. When she finishes with a contented "check," Kevin smiles, noting how relaxed he's become. Molly smiles too. She feels heard, known, and closer to her partners than before.

Heather feels like going last, so Kevin takes his turn. He always starts with how he's currently feeling, because that's usually what is at the front of his mind, so he talks about feeling relaxed and happy. He mentions being hungry and Molly twinkles in agreement. Then he talks about some of the things that have been going through his head for the past few days. An emotional issue comes up; he realizes his feelings were hurt during an interaction with Molly earlier in the day. He shares his feelings and thoughts, noting that he doesn't know more yet and is still processing. As he continues, he finds his mind going down paths where daily life rarely takes it, and ends up saying things he hadn't realized were on his mind before. All the while, Kevin feels safe, knowing that he is being heard and seen but not judged. He eventually runs out of things to say. He feels lighter, like a burden has been lifted. He finishes with "check!"

His partners are looking at him, smiling. It's Heather's turn now, so she begins talking. Once again, the others listen. Heather talks about how her feet hurt from all the dancing she's done recently. She mentions a game she played with her friends earlier, how much fun she had, and how happy it made her to win. She talks about making spaghetti for dinner. Nothing serious or emotional surfaces for her, but she enjoys the opportunity to talk about her day uninterrupted.

When the check-in is over, they will eat dinner. They'll go about their evening as they normally would, but with a greater clarity and understanding of each other's feelings and mental space. This process will enrich their lives together. They will know each other better and feel more connected to one another.

But for now, they simply listen.

Checking in might feel uncomfortable at first. When it's your turn, you may feel stage fright, like you're on the spot. Sometimes people give an impromptu speech rather than actually checking in. You'll get more out of a check-in if you are sharing rather than performing. We suggest starting with people you're comfortable with so you can work through this fear. Also, checking in feels much more natural after some practice. Once you do it a few times, it will become a new pattern of communication, just like conversation is a pattern of communication. In fact, conversation is most people's *only* pattern of communication, so it can be tough to break out of it. Give yourself time and take it easy. It's worth it.

A good way to make checking an even safer space is to agree on the following: everyone will explicitly ask for permission to bring up a subject mentioned in the check-in, and it's completely okay for the person who first brought it up to decline. This applies to both the remainder of the check-in process and afterwards, when normal conversation has resumed. This agreement can help everyone feel even more comfortable bringing up touchy subjects, because it keeps the check-in from becoming a conversation. Perhaps you're not ready for a full-on conversation or argument about a certain topic, but you'd like to let the other person know your half-formed thoughts and feelings. This way, even if you know your words might trigger difficult emotions for those listening, it's still safe to share them because you know no one will attack you. Your check-in partners are listening to you and hearing you, not judging you or attacking you.

Consider it as the listener, too: wouldn't you rather hear what's going on in the other person's head and heart, even if they're not yet ready to engage in conversation about it? Wouldn't that increase your understanding of them and decrease your chance of being blindsided by something you didn't know was on their mind? Checking in is a valuable tool to keep people in touch with each other.

Checking in needn't be reserved for difficult issues; you may wish to make it a daily or weekly practice with your partner. We've found that this improves our communication and our connection. Even in a regularly scheduled check-in, there's no pressure to say anything if you're not ready, don't have anything to say, or are simply not in the mood. You can simply say "check" as the entirety of your turn.

Checking in helps you get in touch with yourself, too! We find that when we check in with each other, especially if we take our time, we discover things inside us that even we didn't know. Checking in is a gift to everyone involved and is a powerful and effective way to create a safe space to share your thoughts and feelings.

CHAPTER 6:

I ALREADY KNOW THIS, BUT

I NEED TO HEAR YOU SAY IT AGAIN

Let's face it, folks: we're scared. Even the most stable and well-adjusted of us are occasionally nervous and insecure. Our work, our friendships, and especially our relationships are plagued by issues, fears, and hangups, and *we need reassurance*. We need to hear "I love you," "I think you're awesome," "I forgive you," or "I appreciate you," even when we've heard it before. Reassurance is no substitute for healthy self-esteem, but even the healthiest of us need to hear it sometimes.

Why is it, then, that we're so afraid of asking for it and so resistant to giving it? It's easy to think, "My friends would never do that to me," or "I'm sure she's got that contract handled," or "I know that he really loves me, no matter what I look like," yet that doesn't always completely quiet our nerves. Verbal reassurance often does help, but realizing that can be scary. When we feel the need for reassurance, we get down on ourselves about it. We deride ourselves for our lack of faith. We criticize ourselves for worrying about something "silly." We're embarrassed to ask because we're afraid of being perceived as weak or of coming across as mistrustful.

That fear is often justified because when *we* are asked for reassurance, we sometimes feel mistrusted. We feel that if our partners really believed us, they wouldn't have to ask.

Why is it so scary to admit that we need reassurance? It's because our culture propagates a very harmful myth: that *we are rational beings.* One of the ways this myth manifests is to make us afraid of asking for reassurance. "I already know this," you might say to yourself. "If I were a better, more rational person, I wouldn't need to ask for reassurance. Asking for this means I'm irrational, inferior, and weak." This is utter nonsense. We are not purely rational beings! We're not computers. We're human beings, and *we're made of meat!* We have hormones and neurotransmitters and all sorts of fluids and goop sloshing around in our bodies, our brains, and our nervous systems. Every one of us has emotions and our emotions don't listen to reason. This isn't wrong or bad. It's the way we're made, and it's okay to be that way. If we can't get our emotions to listen to reason, that doesn't mean we've failed in some way. It means that our emotional side is acting in accordance with its nature.

The solution is to get all this out in the open. Say out loud, *"I already know this, but I need to hear you say it again."* The first half, "I already know this," reassures the other person that it's not about them; It's not about being doubted or mistrusted. The second half, "I need to hear you say it again," asks for what we need — what our emotional, non-rational side needs.

Kyeli's Story: Blammo!

I'm minding my own business, checking my email. A friend emails me to ask how our relationship is going and makes a comment about me "taming the wild Pace." Suddenly, I'm worried that Pace is unhappy or feels trapped in our relationship. **Blammo!** All at once, I'm scared and worried, because this is a touchy issue for me.

I could freak out. I could try to remind myself over and over that she's happy and fine... except that hearing it from myself isn't particularly effective. Or I could call Pace and say "Hey, I got an email that sparked some fear and I'm feeling scared. Can you reassure me that you're happy with me and our relationship? I know it's true, but it would help me to hear it from you." And she will. She'll tell me all the good things and remind me of her joy and the choices she's made to be with me. She'll tell me she loves me, and offer hugs when she gets home. Then the fear will be gone and I'll feel great!

Pace will feel great, too, because she's been given the chance to help me feel safe about something that scares me. It's a win/win situation! The alternative, *not* asking for reassurance, would lead to me having a bad day, feeling scared and fragile, and might even lead to an argument later on.

Being asked for reassurance also gives you an opportunity to be useful, to actively help your partner. You may feel important, needed, loved, and trusted that your partner has opened up to you by asking for what they need.

Another fantastic thing about asking for reassurance is that it gives others permission to ask for reassurance too. When you embrace the non-rational, emotional part of yourself, you send the message that it's okay to have parts that aren't rational, it's okay to be made of meat, and it's okay to ask for what you need. Reassurance is a great way to get your comfort and security needs met when anything upsets your inner balance.

CHAPTER 7:

WHAT PROBLEM ARE YOU

TRYING TO SOLVE?

S ometimes we get caught up in a conversation and forget
our original motivation. We've found that it often helps
to ask, *"What problem are you trying to solve?"*

Pace's Story: Don Needs a Widget

One day at work, my coworker Don came to my
office to ask me for help.

Don: "Hi, Pace, we need you to drop everything you're doing and make changes to Widget A!"

Me: "Hold on a sec, what problem are you trying to solve?"

Don: "Well, we need Widget A to do deduction..."

Me: "Why do you need Widget A in particular?"

Don: "Hmm, well, I guess any widget would do, actually..."

Me: "Could you use Widget B instead? It already exists, and does deduction and more!"

Don: "That's great, we'll use Widget B instead, thanks!"

It's not always quite that simple, but situations like this happen at work *all the time.* People get caught up in the details and lose sight of the big picture. They forget what problem they're trying to solve. By asking what problem they're trying to solve, you can help them with the big picture instead of a detail. This works in relationships, too:

Steve's Example: Fred Needs Quality Time

Steve is a night owl. He works afternoons, so is up much later than his partner Fred. Fred works 8 to 5 and has become frustrated at the difference in their schedules.

Fred: "Steve, I need you to come to bed by 11 on weeknights."

Steve: "I'd really rather not. That's too early for me."

Fred: "It's important to me. I need you to be in bed by 11."

Steve: "Alright, but why? What problem are you trying to solve?"

Fred: "Well, I feel like the only quality time we have these days is when we're cuddling and talking right before bed. I need more of that."

Steve: "Okay, honey, let's talk about that. Maybe we can figure out some ways to get some more quality time together during the afternoons."

Think about what would have happened if the people in those examples would have simply acquiesced to the initial request. If Pace had said, "Sure, I'll get right on those changes to Widget A," or if Steve had said, "Sure, I'll be happy to adjust my sleep schedule a little," none of the people involved would have gotten to the root of the problem. If you fix the symptom instead of fixing the disease, more symptoms will crop up in the future. Pace's coworker might have needed an additional feature that Widget B already had. Fred might have asked for additional things from Steve, without ever fulfilling his need for quality time. Asking "What problem are you trying to solve?" can help everyone involved see the big picture and understand the situation more clearly.

Kyeli's Story: What Are We *Doing?*

Pace and I were discussing a conflict in our plans for the weekend and it escalated into a heated argument. We were both feeling upset and unhappy, and had lost sight of the original issue. In the middle of an angry sentence, Pace stopped and said, "Wait a minute. What problem are we trying to solve?"

I paused. She paused. We both started thinking. After a while, I said, "Well, my feelings were hurt when you snapped at me. When I talked about it, it seemed to make you defensive and I felt attacked again. I reacted with anger and we escalated into this. But all that happened after we resolved our schedule conflict. We solved that problem during the first ten minutes of the conversation, though. So I guess at this point there really isn't a problem, but I'm still feeling hurt and upset."

She put her hand on my arm, looked into my eyes, and said, "I'm sorry. I did get defensive because I knew I'd hurt your feelings and I felt bad. That wasn't fair. I'm sorry and I love you."

At that point, we were able to *stop arguing*. She gave me further reassurance, we held each other, and we went on with our evening and had a lovely time of it. The original problem had long since been solved. The only remaining issues, our emotional states, were easily soothed with kindness and reassurance. Without asking what problem we were trying to solve, she and I might have argued much longer or gotten even more upset!

It isn't always easy to figure out what problem you're trying to solve. It may take some time to uncover the underlying issues behind a conflict. The root is often underground. Be patient with yourself and your partner, because taking the time to find those roots will yield deeper, more lasting solutions.

Asking what problem you're trying to solve is a simple, effective way of cutting through a potential argument or misunderstanding. It gets to the root of the problem and enables you and your partner to focus on the real issues instead of the symptoms. This allows for richer, happier communication!

Chapter 8:

Feeling considered

Feeling considered is knowing that someone has thought of you and respected your wishes when making their own plans. When we consider someone else, we take into account how they feel, what they are thinking, and what they may need before we go ahead with our plans. It's different from asking permission. Asking permission is seeking approval, but consideration extends an invitation to your partner to be a part of what you're doing, even in a small way. It is often as simple as rephrasing "I am going to do this" to "I would like to do this" or "Would you mind if I did this?"

Kyeli's Story: The Road Trip

Pace and I were going on a road trip. As we headed to the car, she said, "I'm going to read my book on the drive." I was instantly annoyed; would I be able to listen to music without bothering her? Conversation would be out, too. My entire trip had now become a little less pleasant and my mood had dipped. It took me a while to get my thoughts and feelings sorted out, so she did indeed read her book while I was processing. After I was in a better place, I asked if we could talk. She agreed, so I told her how I felt: when she stated she was going to read, I felt unconsidered. I felt like she didn't take my needs or wants into account; she decided what she wanted to do and stated she was going to do it.

In talking about my feelings, I wound up pushing one of her buttons. She felt like I was saying she had to ask permission to read. That wasn't my intent at all! I needed consideration, not to be asked for permission. I told her, if she said, "Do you mind if I read during the drive?" or even "I'd like to read on the drive," I would have felt like she was giving me total consideration. She would have been checking with me to see if I had any reasons for her not doing so. The likelihood would be that she'd still get what she wanted and I would be happy because I was considered. It's not that I didn't want her to read; I wanted to know that she was thinking of me when she made plans. She understood and agreed to be more considerate in the future.

If you don't consider your partner, they may feel hurt like Kyeli did. If you do consider your partner, chances are it will be a win/win situation. Your partner will have no objection, will feel cared for, and you will still get what you want. If your partner *does* have an objection, that's an opportunity for communication and you can work things out with no hurt feelings.

Rebeka's Example: Music vs. Video

Rebeka and her partner Tammi both work from home, so the time they're online often overlaps. They work on separate computers in the same room during the day. Rebeka usually checks with Tammi before playing music, to be sure it won't bother her.

One day, Rebeka had her music playing and Tammi started watching a video. Rebeka found this loud and disruptive. She said sarcastically, "Well, I guess I'll just turn my music off, then." Catching her own passive-aggressive behavior, she waited until Tammi's video ended and asked if they could talk it out. "Sure," said Tammi.

Rebeka asked Tammi, "In the future could you please ask before watching a video with sound when I'm playing music? Two sounds happening at once is distracting for me."

Tammi replied, "Sure, I'm fine with asking you first, as long as sometimes you're willing to turn off your music instead, or put on headphones if there's a video I want to watch."

Rebeka agreed. They both felt happy and considered, and they were able to work together with less stress in the future.

Feeling considered is important. We all want to feel like our loved ones are thinking of us. When they make their own plans without considering us first, we can feel ignored, slighted, or devalued, which leads to hurt feelings. Usually our loved ones aren't actually ignoring or devaluing us, but feeling that way is never pleasant. It's delightful that this problem can easily be sidestepped by considering our partners and rephrasing our words to better reflect our intentions!

PART II:
BOUNDARIES

CHAPTER 9:

HOLDING HEALTHY BOUNDARIES

Boundaries are tricky things. By "boundaries," we're not referring to lines on maps or fences in fields; we mean the boundaries of responsibility.

Becky's Example: Too Late for the Show

Becky made plans to see a movie with Wes at 4:30 on Saturday. They agree on a time and a theater a week in advance. On Friday, they have a conversation:

Wes: "Hey Becky, could we do dinner tomorrow?"

Becky: "Sure, how about Clay Pit at 8?"

Wes: "Sounds good."

On Saturday, Becky shows up at the theater and Wes is nowhere to be seen. She calls him to ask where he is.

Becky: "Hi Wes, are you running late?"

Wes: "What? It's only 4:30, and we're not eating until 8, right?"

Becky: "Right, but we were going to see a movie at 4:30."

Wes: "I thought we were having dinner *instead of* the movie. If we were doing both, I wouldn't have expected you to suggest a time, and I wouldn't have expected the time to be so long after the end of the movie."

Becky: "Oh, I thought we would have dinner in addition to the movie. We never canceled our movie plans, so I assumed they were still on. I guess we miscommunicated."

Wes: "I guess we did."

Becky and Wes had a misunderstanding about their plans. They each made the usual error; they filled in the gaps in the conversation with their own assumptions. Does Becky place the responsibility on Wes for misunderstanding her, or does she take the responsibility upon herself for not having been clear enough? In other words, where do they draw their boundaries?

Imagine your boundaries of responsibility as a circle around yourself. You take responsibility for the things inside the circle, and you let others take responsibility for what's outside.

If you pull your boundaries too far in, you become an island. Imagine standing up and hugging your arms to yourself. There's no room for anyone else in there — you're shutting others out! You're living in your own little shell. You're not fully present in the world because you're wearing emotional armor.[1] If you're an island, you take less than your share of responsibility because you feel protected and isolated. This results in the usual error: things don't hurt you because of your armor, but you forget that others aren't wearing armor like yours, and that they *can* get hurt. Thus, you may neglect to take responsibility for the way your words and actions might impact others.

On the other end of the spectrum, if you have your boundaries too far out, you'll take on far more responsibility than is rightfully yours to take. Imagine standing up and holding your arms out as wide open as you can. There's way too much room inside those boundaries! Now you're taking on responsibility for *everyone* who can fit in your boundaries: their reactions, emotions, thoughts and feelings become *your* responsibility, so you may feel like you must choose every word and action very carefully to avoid hurting anyone.

Now imagine standing up, this time with your arms outstretched enough to make a reasonable circle. You're not shutting everyone out, but you're not letting everyone in, either. You're *holding healthy boundaries* and allowing others to do the same. You're taking responsibility for your words and actions. You're

---

1   For a beautiful story about emotional armor, read *The Knight In Rusty Armor* by Robert Fisher.

taking all the responsibility that is yours and no more, and you're being mindful of where you draw the line. In this way, you can communicate and interact much more helpfully and effectively.

Kyeli's Story:

Rate Your Cleanliness on a Scale from 1 to 10

We had some friends coming in from out of town. One of them is considerably more of a neat freak than either Pace or myself, so we discussed the state of our apartment at length before he bought his plane ticket. We certainly wanted him to be comfortable while visiting, but we weren't willing to kill ourselves cleaning. Pace made a scale from one to ten (one being a pig's sty, ten being a hospital), calibrated the scale by numbering places they'd both been, marked our place as usually a five or six, and asked what he would prefer. He said a seven would be great and we agreed. We reached a wonderful compromise.

Then, a few days after the conversation, Pace was worried that he would be upset when he got here if our idea of seven didn't match his. I reminded her that the two of them had discussed it clearly, terms had been stated, and all had agreed. If he got here and felt dissatisfied, that wasn't our responsibility, because we'd done all we could to accommodate him. Now, if we'd decided to ignore his requests and leave the apartment as it was, then it would be our responsibility if he got upset, but that wasn't what was happening.

We weren't an island: we didn't tell him to suck it up and deal with a messier place than he'd be comfortable in. We weren't too giving, either: we didn't spend weeks making the place absolutely spotless. We were in the happy medium: we cleaned up enough to make him comfortable. We then trusted him to be responsible for himself and to let us know if he needed anything while he was here.

As it turned out, everything went wonderfully and all of us were very happy.

Holding healthy boundaries is vital for healthy, happy relationships. When you take responsibility for others, you're taking that responsibility away from them and denying them the chance to find their own boundaries. It can be hard to let others take their share of the responsibility for their lives, but they'll never have the chance if you keep taking it away from them. At the same time, pulling your boundaries in too far creates difficulty in relating to others, as well as a lack of compassion and connection. There's a fine line between giving too much and giving too little, but it's worth the effort to find the happy medium. In addition, holding healthy boundaries and maintaining them firmly when they are challenged tends to attract people who also hold healthy boundaries. By giving others the opportunity to be responsible adults, we attract those who choose to take advantage of that opportunity.

Chapter 10:

Fierceness

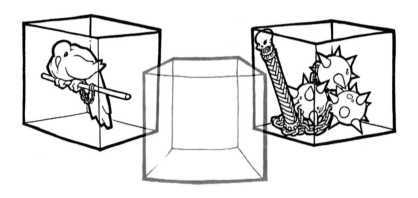

O ur culture holds the illusion that there are only two ways to be: peaceful or violent. If you are peaceful, it's not acceptable to stand up for yourself when someone crosses your boundaries. Peaceful people don't rock the boat. Peaceful people obey authority. Peaceful people will go to any lengths to avoid conflict and appease those who are angry.

Your alternative is to be violent. Violent people aren't nice. Violent people don't respect the boundaries of others. Our society sometimes has a kind of sick worship of violent people, like ancient conquerors or CEOs who cut employee health plans to pad their own retirement funds. Violent people don't necessarily cause physical harm, but they do whatever it takes to get their way, crushing whomever stands in their path. For ordinary people, however, it's unacceptable to be violent.

This game is rigged! We've been offered the "choice" to go into either of these two boxes: the peaceful box or the violent box. The peaceful box sings of niceness, happiness, calmness; who would want to go into the violent box? Only bad people go in there. It's a bait and switch. We choose the peaceful box, but the baggage that comes along is passivity, obedience, and complacency. We learn that it's wrong to stand up for ourselves, and if we do, we're often called mean, harsh, or cruel, and put into the violent box.

Luckily, there is a third box: *fierceness.* Peaceful is complacent, violent is aggressive, but fierce is the middle ground: *assertive.* Being fierce is being passionate about what you believe, defending your boundaries, and getting what you need without disrespecting others. It's standing up for yourself without knocking down everyone else. We're taught that fierceness equals violence, but that's simply not true. Consider Gandhi; his actions as a leader illustrate fierceness. Gandhi wasn't violent, but he certainly wasn't peaceful in the sense we're told we have to be; he wasn't complacent or mindlessly obedient, nor was he aggressive or disrespectful. He stated his boundaries clearly and stood his ground firmly when they were crossed.

Gryphon's Story:

The Clawless Swipe of Fierceness

Like most cats, our kitten Gryphon excels at setting and keeping good boundaries. If someone violates Gryphon's boundaries, he will let them know with a hiss and a clawless swipe: nonverbal communication for "The line is drawn and you have crossed it." If the offender backs off, ceases the offensive action, and takes care to avoid violating Gryphon's boundaries again, they'll be fine. In fact, if they treat him with respect they'll eventually earn his trust. Otherwise, if they continue to violate his boundaries, they'll get hurt.

We can learn a lot from how cats communicate and defend their boundaries. They communicate their boundaries with a hiss and a clawless swipe, clearly expressing what will happen if the line is crossed again.

If someone violates a boundary you have clearly expressed, warn them that the line has been crossed and explain the consequences of a repeat offense. If they persist in disrespecting your boundary, fiercely defend yourself by either fixing the situation or removing yourself from it.

Kyeli's Story: Improv Night

I worked for a theater instructor named Eduardo a few years ago. One night, we hosted an improv event for his students. Since it was a family friendly event, I had my eight-year-old son Dru with me. At one point, Dru and a couple of other boys played quietly in the back of the building while Eduardo performed on stage. The boys kept quiet, so I left them alone. However, after his skit, Eduardo flew to the back of the building and descended upon Dru. As soon as he walked away, I went to Dru to see what had happened. Dru said Eduardo had told him that he was being too distracting and that he wanted Dru to either quit playing or go outside.

After making sure Dru was okay, I pulled Eduardo aside to talk about what had happened. I told him that he was totally out of line. I found it unacceptable that he told my son to go out and play in a parking lot in the dark without talking to me first. I explained how very upset I felt. He apologized in a flippant tone and seemed to think that was the end of it, but I still felt angry. It seemed like he hadn't heard me at all!

I tried harder to clearly convey my feelings, but after a few minutes he said, "I apologized, I said I wouldn't do it again, no one was hurt, what more do you want? We have a business relationship. What happened with your kid doesn't come into it. Let it go so we can continue to work together."

I replied, "My son is a part of everything I do. By endangering him, you endanger our work relationship." He, however, continued to dodge responsibility and even refused to reassure me that similar things wouldn't happen again. I took a couple of deep breaths and made a decision. I said, "No. I will work the rest of this week, because you have already paid me. But Friday afternoon, I am done. This is over. I won't work with you anymore."

I have a clear boundary: do not ever endanger the life of my child. When my boss crossed this boundary and then refused to acknowledge it, I stood up for myself and my son. I became fierce and took my family away from the potential of future dangerous situations.

In communication, especially during conflict, we often take on the roles of peaceful or violent. One person takes the role of the attacker (violent) and the other one either meekly apologizes (peaceful) or fights back (violent). These roles block healthy communication. If you take the violent role, you may feel good about standing up for what you need, but you may also feel guilty for hurting someone else in order to fill your needs. If you take the peaceful role, you may feel good about having avoided conflict, but you may also feel disappointed or bitter about not getting your needs met.

You don't have to take either of those roles; instead, you can be fierce. Communicating with fierceness means asking for what you need while respecting the needs of your partner. Fierceness empowers you to clearly communicate your boundaries and to stand up for yourself if your partner crosses any of them. When you act fiercely, you are better able to treat yourself and your partner with equal respect.

Many people are at a loss when encountering fierceness because it's still all too rare. Just as it's vital to protect your physical boundaries, it's important to defend your emotional and conversational boundaries. Fierceness takes practice and can be nerve-wracking or frustrating, but it's well worth the effort. Once you learn where your boundaries are and can communicate them effectively, fierceness empowers you to protect those boundaries without feeling overly meek or overly destructive.

CHAPTER 11:

ASK FOR WHAT YOU NEED

"If you really loved me, you would just know!"

This sentiment reflects one of the most harmful myths of communication. This myth prevents useful communication from taking place and leads to expectations that no one could possibly meet. The broken expectations that follow cause hurt and pain. If we pull back the curtain of this myth to look behind it, we will see the truth: *no one can read your mind.*

When we grow close to someone, we sometimes feel like we merge together into one person. We've seen many of our friends treat couples as if they were one person with the same wants and needs. It happens on the inside of a relationship, too. We sometimes feel that the level of closeness we have achieved will somehow let us merge our minds together. If that were possible, we'd have written a book on mind-merging instead of a book on communication! The only way to make your wants and needs known is to communicate clearly and openly: to *ask for what you need.*

For example, take a wife who wishes her husband would occasionally buy her flowers. She talks with her friends and complains about her husband. "He just doesn't understand me," she says. "If he really loved me and really knew me, he would know what I want." Her friends will console her and commiserate with her, because they all buy into the myth. She doesn't even consider *asking* him for flowers or *telling* him what she wants, because that would feel like giving in. She feels that if she has to ask, it somehow doesn't count. That would be losing the "he can read my mind" game. If she loses this game, she doesn't get

what she wants, but she feels *justified* in being disappointed, because this is the way the game is played.

This is a game with no winners! No matter what expectations she has, he's not going to read her mind. He doesn't have an opportunity to make her happy and she's setting herself up to be disappointed. Why on earth do we do this?

Here's what might happen if she asked for what she wanted:

"Honey, it would make me really happy if you would occasionally buy me flowers. It would make me feel loved, considered, and appreciated," she tells her husband.

"Oh! I didn't know you liked flowers. I'd be more than happy to," he replies. He buys her flowers the very next day.

She feels surprised that she appreciates the flowers as much as she would have if she had received them as a spontaneous gift. She expected that it wouldn't count if she had to ask for it, but that was another part of the harmful myth she used to buy into. By communicating with her husband and asking for what she wanted, she was happy instead of disappointed.

Kyeli's Story: Let's Talk About Text, Baby!

When Pace is working, she hyperfocuses to the exclusion of everything else. I felt like she would go to work and completely forget about me for eight hours a day, to the point of resenting me for any interruptions. I didn't like feeling that way; I needed to feel special to her during those hours. I felt afraid to ask for attention, because she reacted with irritation when interrupted from her "work mode."

I spent a long time talking to everyone but Pace about this situation. Several of our friends kept suggesting I talk to Pace, that I ask for what I need from her, but I was stubborn. Finally, a friend dared me to try asking her anyway. If it devalued anything Pace did for me, what would I be losing? My needs weren't being met as things were, so it couldn't get much worse, right?

I worked up the nerve to talk to Pace about it. We agreed that text messages on our phones were a great way to communicate that she was thinking of me. However, I was sure that it would feel artificial, since I'd specifically asked for it.

The first time she texted me, all she said was "I love you!" but it *totally made my day!* I felt loved, special, and considered. I saved the message and went back to look at it occasionally for the rest of the day.

I asked for what I needed and when I got it, it was no less special for the asking! Who knew?

In reality, the two choices we have in these sorts of situations are: 1) We can wait for others to read our minds and be disappointed and bitter when they fail to meet those unreasonable expectations, or 2) we can ask for what we want or need and at least have a chance of getting it. We advocate choice 2.

Sometimes it's hard to ask for what we need. We may get attached to the idea of our partners figuring out what we need and surprising us with it, so we build up a lot of resistance to asking. Sometimes the source of this resistance is shame. We may (consciously or subconsciously) feel ashamed of our needs or feel that we don't deserve to have our needs met. These feelings can bog us down, preventing us from asking for what we need.

Fear of rejection can also bog us down. We may feel like we would rather suffer quietly than risk being turned down. Complete and total rejection hurts bitterly, but in our experience it's more rare than our fears make it out to be. Usually we can turn the initial rejection into a compromise with some patience and communication.

Kyeli's Story: Buy Me a Present!

My primary love language[1] is receiving gifts. Pace, however, hates shopping and feels stressed at the very idea.

When I expressed my need to receive presents from her, she initially rejected me. Once we dealt with my hurt feelings, we were able to compromise. I now keep an up-to-date, easily accessible wish list

---

1   Love languages are neat and helpful to know about. We recommend reading *The Five Love Languages* by Gary Chapman.

(to remove the guesswork) and she guarantees me gifts on at least three occasions: my birthday, our anniversary, and Yule.

This way, my needs are at least partially met without causing her constant stress. It works well for both of us, and is far better than the way things were before I asked for what I needed.

We're going to offer you a challenge. Remember this challenge the next time you want or need something, but you're afraid of rejection or you feel like asking for it would devalue it. The challenge is: *ask anyway.* Try it and see how you feel; see if the asking actually does devalue the receiving. The results may surprise you.

However it works for you, find a way to ask for what you need. Expecting your partner to read your mind is unrealistic and unkind to both of you. Getting your needs met requires clear and direct communication.

Chapter 12:

I am not green

We often find it difficult to believe compliments. Someone offers one and we make excuses or noises of embarrassed gratitude. A compliment to our clothing results in "This old thing?" A compliment to our hair produces a startled, "I didn't do anything to it!" We brush it off. We don't believe it. We don't take it to heart.

On the other hand, someone throws a critical comment at us and it sticks like glue in our minds, often long after our critic has forgotten the off-handed remark. A casual "What happened to your hair today?" can make us want a haircut immediately. "Have you gained a little weight?" sends us spiraling into doubt and fear, and can even spark self-abusive weight loss cycles.

It's not just our appearance that's subject to such frightful scrutiny; our personalities are just as vulnerable. We get into an argument with a partner, and they spout a particularly hurtful comment. Suddenly, we're hurt or angry; whatever we were feeling has been amplified. Doubt creeps in, and we think, "Am I really like that?"

The answer is simple: no, you're not.

The person saying those hurtful words isn't actually talking about *you*. They're talking about *their perception of you,* filtered through their own issues, paradigm, and opinions. These opinions often fluctuate when anger takes control.

It's like a little voodoo doll created to look vaguely like you. When that person says hurtful things, they're not directly hurting you. They're making statements about their concept of you, which is often very different from the actual you. They're sticking pins in that voodoo doll and you're saying "Ouch!" but it only hurts if you believe that the voodoo doll is *actually you.* For cases where the hurtful person doesn't know what they're talking about, you can break the chain of hurt by breaking the link between you and the voodoo doll.

Kyeli's Story: Drawing Down the Lightning

When my friend Margaret was going through some major life changes, her brother Paul treated me badly. He was scared, felt like he was losing Margaret, and needed someone to foot the blame. He chose me to bear the brunt of his attacks because I was fiercely protecting her and was an easy target. I don't actually remember the things he said, but I certainly remember the feelings his words inspired in me: fear, hurt, sorrow, self-doubt. I was letting him have power over me, letting his words control my emotions, even letting him affect my self-image!

Pace and I talked about this a lot. Pace said that Paul wasn't actually attacking *me;* he was attacking a voodoo doll of me and I was saying "Ouch!" every time he stuck a pin in. That made sense, but was hard for me to fully understand. Later, another friend said that it was like Paul was saying I was green. However, I'm *not* actually green, and no amount of him saying so would make it true.

Suddenly, all the talk of voodoo dolls and weird colors sunk in — *I am not green!*

When Paul got angry, he needed to vent. I was loud and on the front line, like a lightning rod, so he got angry at me. He made me his scapegoat. I felt hurt and scared. I gave him power over me when I allowed his words to hurt me. Then I realized that what matters most is how we see ourselves. Having a strong sense of self enables us to avoid letting other people have power over us, in anger or in any situation.

When we get into arguments, tempers flare. Sometimes we say things we don't mean, or our partner says things they don't mean. Once something has been said, it's not easy to let go or forget. We have a tendency to hold tightly to the hurtful things someone says about us long after the anger has dissipated. Sometimes, those insidious words will linger in our minds for a long time, months or even years, and can damage our self-esteem. For example, if someone says, "You can't write worth a damn!" in the heat of an argument, the next time you sit down to write, you may think about that. Your ability to write may be affected by the harsh words of another person, even when those words are completely untrue!

Next time someone says hurtful things to you, imagine they're saying you're green or sticking pins in a voodoo doll made to look like you. Feel the separation between you — the actual you that you are — and your attacker's perception of you. If you vividly imagine the person being insulted as someone other than your actual self (a voodoo doll, a green person, or something else clearly *not you*), it can help you feel that separation. Feeling the separation empowers you and enables you to avoid taking harsh words too personally. More than likely, it's not even about you. As in Kyeli's story, the other person is probably saying those words for their own reasons rather than because the words are true.

CHAPTER 13:

"I" STATEMENTS

How many times have you initiated a simple conversation, only to have it somehow turn into an argument? This often happens when we feel like our partner has crossed our boundaries, and we feel attacked or accused. *"I" statements* — statements about oneself and one's feelings — help avoid this problem.

Using "you" statements:

Gretchen: "*You* hurt me when you left without telling me where you were going."

Zack: "Well, I wouldn't have done that if *you* hadn't made me angry."

Using "I" statements:

Gretchen: "*I* felt hurt when you left without telling me where you were going."

Zack: "I'm sorry you felt hurt; that wasn't my intent. *I* was feeling angry and upset."

When we use "you" statements, our partners often feel threatened and react with defensiveness. "You" statements feel like attacks. If instead we use "I" statements and talk about our feelings and reactions to a situation, we are much less likely to provoke a defensive reaction. It's hard to argue against someone else's feelings!

Kyeli's Story: In My Perspective

When someone uses a "you" statement, I often feel like they're talking *at* me. I feel attacked and immediately go on the defensive. It's then difficult for any real communication to happen, and it's hard for me to calm down enough to listen.

If, on the other hand, someone speaks to me with "I" statements, I can hear what they're communicating without my emotions flaring. I feel drawn in; I find myself sympathetic and willing to listen and make things better!

My favorite phrase in these situations is "in my perspective." It calls attention to the fact that we all have different communication styles, and reminds whomever I'm speaking with that what I say comes from my personal perspective. I often follow these statements up with something like, "I realize your perspective might be different, but this is how it was for me."

So much more communication happens this way!

Some phrases that may be useful to replace with an "I" statement:

"You hurt me..."

"You made me..."

"You are..."

"What *really* happened was..."

Some useful phrases to help you rephrase things as "I" statements:

"I feel..."

"In my perspective, ..."

"For me, ..."

"I remember..."

The goal of "I" statements is to avoid provoking a defensive reaction. If you only talk about your own feelings, your own perceptions, your own actions, and your own reactions, there's no room for argument. Your feelings are what they are, regardless of why you feel them or how your partner feels about them. Your perceptions are what they are, regardless of whether you perceived things accurately. You are the sole expert on yourself; if you say, "This is how I feel," no one can reasonably disagree with you and so there's no opportunity for a conflict to begin. Your partner may feel you are overreacting or being overly emotional, but you'll find more common ground for reaching resolution if you communicate openly about what your feelings *are* rather than what anyone expects them to be.

Here are some ways *not* to use "I" statements.

A "you" statement posing as an "I" statement:

Gretchen: "I felt like you were being a real jerk when you walked out without telling me where you were going."

Zack: "Oh yeah? Well, in my perspective, you can be a real bitch sometimes!"

Just inserting "I felt" or "in my perspective" into a sentence does *not* mean you're using "I" statements. The point of "I" statements is the intent, not the syntax. If you speak about your point of view and your feelings without attempting to impose your viewpoint on the other person, then you're really using "I" statements.

Here's an example of a situation where an "I" statement is *not* the best response:

Sometimes the best response is a "you" statement.

Zack: *(punches Gretchen in the face)*

Gretchen: "I felt hurt and bruised when you punched me in the face."

No! In this case, there is an actual attack instead of a perceived attack. Using an "I" statement like Gretchen's would set your boundaries too far out; it would let the attacker off the hook by taking the responsibility away from him and onto you. A better response would be, "You hurt and bruised me badly when you punched me in the face and I'm not going to take that from you anymore." When someone does something that directly hurts us, a "you" statement is most appropriate. Outright physical abuse certainly warrants a "you" statement, as does verbal abuse.

The best response to verbal abuse is also a "you" statement.

Gretchen: "You're a filthy, lazy, pathetic, worthless ass and I wish you had never been born!"

Zack: "I felt hurt when you said all those mean things."

No! Just like in the example with the physical attack, this "I" statement takes the responsibility from the attacker, where it belongs, and puts it onto you. A better response would be something fierce like "That's verbal abuse. If you say anything like that again, I'm walking right out that door."

"I" statements are another example of holding healthy boundaries. It's good to take responsibility for your own feelings; in most cases (but not all), "I" statements are useful and appropriate. Using "I" statements authentically and in the right circumstances can defuse volatile situations, allowing both partners to communicate clearly without provoking defensiveness.

CHAPTER 14:

IT'S NOT ALL ABOUT ME

The root cause of the usual error is that we assume things about others based on our own internal perceptions, concepts, and experiences. In addition to causing the usual error, this causes another error: the *egocentric bias*. We know everything there is to know about our own actions and responses, so we mistakenly assume we're responsible for the actions and responses of others. For instance, when someone we know is upset and we don't know the cause, we're more likely to think it's because of something we did than to think it's because of something completely unrelated.

Kyeli's Story: The Urgent Email

One morning, I launched into an argument with Pace before she left for work. Later in the morning, I wrote her an email explaining to her the reason I'd been upset. It was a touchy subject for me, so I was a little nervous about sending the email. We do like to talk about things, though, so I sent it.

By lunchtime, I'd heard nothing from her. I was getting nervous.

By the time she came home, I was a huge mess of nerves. She came in and was grouchy and didn't feel like talking about anything right away. We had dinner and watched an episode of *Buffy the Vampire Slayer* while I worked myself into a frenzy.

Finally, she said she was feeling better, so I asked if we could talk. She said sure, so I asked if my email had upset her.

She looked puzzled, then laughed. "No! I meant to reply to you and tell you everything is totally fine, but I had a *horrible* day at work and was super busy and didn't have any time to do anything but work all day!"

I'd gotten frantically worried over nothing because I spent the day thinking it was all about me, when really it wasn't about me at all!

Another way this manifests is in the way we relate the events of our lives to ourselves. A car crashes on the highway, causing traffic to come to a standstill, and we say to ourselves, "Why did this have to happen to *me?*"

Thinking of events only in terms of how they relate to us causes us to miss out on the bigger picture. If someone cuts us off on the road, we think, "What a jerk, cutting me off like that," attributing malice or callousness to what could simply be mistake or necessity. We don't think of the possibility that they simply missed us when checking their blind spot, or that they had to change lanes quickly to avoid someone suddenly slowing in their lane, or that some mechanical or medical condition may be impairing their driving.

This isn't because of any moral flaw on our part; it's an effect of our necessarily self-focused worldview. The bad news is that it tends to cause far more stress and disappointment than happiness. The good news is that we aren't trapped by this! We can take steps to mitigate this bias and its effects on us. We can remind ourselves, *"It's not all about me."*

This phrase isn't meant to chastise or diminish ourselves; it's a reminder that even though your internal world *is* all about you, the external world is not. It reminds us to expand our view and look outside of our own scope so we can see things more clearly, improve our lives, and be happier.

Pace's Story: Kyeli's Kidney Stone

A few years ago, Kyeli suffered through a year of painful, debilitating, and frustrating medical difficulties. As a result, she built up a lot of residual anger, fear, pain, and bitterness that caused mood swings. She had occasional outbursts of sadness or rage.

When she had one of those outbursts around me, especially if it happened during a conversation, I immediately jumped to the conclusion that *I* must have done something to cause her sadness or upset — but it wasn't true. Even if my words or actions happened to trigger an outburst, that didn't mean I *caused* the outburst.

Reminding myself that it wasn't all about me helped bring me to my senses when I felt like I was the cause of her emotions. If I had gotten stuck in feeling like it was about me, I would have been lost in a blamestorm and made the situation even more difficult for both Kyeli and myself. When I remembered that it wasn't all about me, I managed to stay calm enough to support her.

Triggers and *landmines* are important examples of "it's not all about me." These are metaphors for our insecurities, our extreme emotional reactions to things, and our "hot-button" issues. Landmines are our deeply buried emotional issues that don't surface on a regular basis. If you have a fear of spiders and your partner playfully pretends their hand is a spider, they may be surprised when you scream. Your partner has stepped on one of your landmines; they have accidentally triggered an extreme and unexpected emotional reaction.

Michelle and Anthony's Example:

It's All About Me

When Michelle was young, her father went on a business trip and never came home. He ran off with another woman and abandoned Michelle completely. The trauma from this experience left Michelle with a severe abandonment trigger.

Today, Michelle's husband Anthony has gone on a business trip alone. Though she is excited for the opportunities this trip gives him, she's now feeling afraid that Anthony will abandon her because her fear has been triggered. She needs reassurance, so she calls him.

Michelle: "Hi! How are you doing, honey?"

Anthony: "I'm having a great trip! I'm having a lot of fun and enjoying myself a lot!"

Michelle: *(holding back tears)* "So you're happier without me around, is that it?!"

Anthony: "What? Where did *that* come from? Why are you upset? You're the one who *wanted* me to go on this trip!"

What happened here? Anthony responded genuinely, sharing his enthusiasm for his trip with Michelle. He didn't have her insecurities on his mind. He accidentally stepped on her landmine, triggering her fear. She responded by lashing out. This is why we call them "landmines": it can often feel like stepping on a landmine. We're casually talking, and all of a sudden **BOOM!** There's a huge explosion! We also call them "triggers" because any innocent word or phrase can trigger the insecurity and the resulting emotional explosion.

When dealing with landmines and triggers, it's especially important to remember that it's not about you. Anthony didn't do anything wrong, and neither did Michelle. Michelle's insecurity was triggered and she reacted emotionally to an issue that she finds scary and difficult. In these situations it's hard not to take it personally, like Anthony did in the previous story. He responded defensively because he felt that Michelle had accused him of doing something wrong. However, that wasn't Michelle's intent. She expressed the emotion triggered by Anthony accidentally stepping on one of her landmines. If Anthony had recognized that Michelle had been triggered and felt afraid, the conversation might have gone differently.

Michelle and Anthony's Example:

It's Not All About Me

Michelle: "Hi! How are you doing, honey?"

Anthony: "I'm having a great trip! I'm having a lot of fun and enjoying myself a lot!"

Michelle: *(holding back tears)* "So you're happier without me around, is that it?!"

Anthony: "What?" *(pauses for thought, realises that he has accidentally stepped on one of Michelle's landmines)* "Not at all, sweetie! I'm sorry that this is triggery for you, and I'll be happy to reassure you as much as you need."

Once a landmine has been stepped on, it's time to do damage control. Aid your partner and reassure them; we often need extra reassurance when our landmines explode. To aid yourself, remind yourself that you've done nothing wrong and remember that it's not about you. This will help you be compassionate and open instead of defensive and upset.

We use "it's not all about me" primarily in communication, but knowing that most things are generally not about you is useful in many other situations as well. When something happens and your initial reaction is one of self-blame or guilt, thinking it over with a broader perspective will help you discover whether it actually is about you. More often than not, you have little or nothing to do with any given situation, and you can save yourself a lot of frustration, stress, and guilt!

Part III:
Turning Conflict
Into Communication

CHAPTER 15:

WHAT DID YOU INTEND?

Communication can be scary and dangerous. We use lethal-sounding words like "landmine" and "trigger" to describe some unpleasant surprises you can stumble upon while communicating. Even in normal conversations about everyday subjects, we sometimes say things that seem totally innocuous to us, and we're blindsided when the other person reacts with anger, hurt, or fear.

It's no fun to be on the other end, either. There you are, having a pleasant conversation, when the person you're talking with suddenly drops a bomb on you, saying something unimaginably hurtful, and then sits there with bug-eyed surprise when you express your hurt feelings! What's going on here?

It's easy to believe that we live in a single, shared, objective world, while in truth we each live in our own personal world of concepts. We each have a minefield of hangups, fears, and issues built on past hurts that cause emotional reactions when we encounter them. Sometimes we react by getting angry or by closing down. No matter how universal or obvious an issue seems to us, other people have different internal landscapes and, therefore, different minefields.

Similarly, we interpret things differently from how they were meant because if we had said them, we would have meant something else. That reason — the one we would have had — is the reason that makes sense to us, so we make the usual error. An issue that is a big deal to us may not be a big deal to someone else; they may have stepped on our landmine entirely by accident.

Here's the simple solution we've found to this problem of mysterious mental minefields: the phrase *"What did you intend?"*

The key to using this phrase effectively is to be aware of the constant potential for the usual error. That's what you're doing by reading this book, so you're on your way already. Then, whenever someone steps on one of your landmines, remember that you have a choice. One choice is to assume your interpretation of their intent is correct, make emotional conclusions, and get angry, upset, or hurt. A second choice is to ask, "What did you intend by that?" People generally like to talk about themselves, so they'll likely give you an explanation of what's happening in their inner world. Asking for clarification gives you both a second chance at successful communication!

People don't usually intend to hurt others when communicating with them, so your strong negative reaction signals that something might have gone wrong in the communication process. You may have a different understanding of the words your partner chose, so you made an assumption about their intent. However, things are almost never as we assume them to be. (If our assumptions were always right, we wouldn't need to communicate in the first place!)

Sometimes it doesn't go so smoothly. Sometimes asking "What did you intend?" elicits defensiveness from your partner. You can almost see the mental backpedaling: "Oh, did I say something wrong? Why is she asking me that? I'm not actually sure what my intent was, so I'd better make something up fast!" If you can see your partner panic or get defensive about the question, explain why you're asking. Say something like, "I don't understand what you meant. What I heard hurt my feelings, but I don't think you intended to hurt me so I probably misunderstood. Can you clarify what you meant?"

We've found that asking "What did you intend?" defuses potential conflicts successfully and makes life a lot less stressful.

That takes care of one side of the issue, but what about the cases where you trip over someone else's landmine? In close relationships, where you and your partner are actively working to communicate better, you can simply share this information. If they like the idea, they can ask you, "What did you intend?" when you step on their landmines.

In other situations, where teaching communication skills isn't seen as socially appropriate, you can take the above advice and use it in reverse. When you step on someone's landmine, keep in mind that the person isn't blowing up at you. They're not freaking out about you, they're not retreating from you. They're reacting to an imaginary you. They're reacting to the "you" in their head who makes the same assumptions they do. If you can remember that, you'll remember that you are not green, and then you can explain your own intent and clear things up before they get out of hand.

Kyell's Story:

Pace Humiliates Me in Front of Our Friends

One afternoon, Pace emailed me to let me know that she would be working late. We already had plans for that night, so I felt disappointed. I emailed the group of friends we were meeting to let them know that she wouldn't be able to make it (including Pace so she could remain in the loop). I used negative, sarcastic expressions to vent my hurt feelings.

Pace replied to the entire group by going through my email, paragraph by paragraph, and rephrasing everything I said in a more positive manner. When I read her email, I felt humiliated, as if Pace were a school teacher who had called me out in front of the whole class. I felt hurt and embarrassed. I was also baffled as to why she would do such a thing to me.

I took a few deep breaths, held my emotions at bay, and waited until she came home. That night, I asked her, "What did you intend by rephrasing my email?" She said she tried to make light of the disappointing situation while showing our friends how excited we were about rephrasing things positively. The previous week, we'd met with the same friends to discuss rephrasing things positively and other communication-related concepts, so she wanted to show them an example of putting it into practice. I told her how I had felt humiliated. That surprised her, because that hadn't been her intent at all. She apologized and hugged me. We discussed the intent behind each of our emails, and we agreed that next time we would do things differently. I felt better knowing her actual intent and she felt better knowing what *my* intent with the original email had been.

In a very real way, asking "What did you intend?" is a gift. It's a gift to yourself, because it can save you from unnecessary pain and confusion. It's a gift to others, because it helps them convey their meaning clearly and without misunderstanding. It's even a gift to be asked, because sometimes we ourselves don't know what we intended. Sometimes we run on autopilot or act based on unconscious issues. When someone asks for clarification about your intent, you might discover more about yourself, and that is an extra bonus gift!

CHAPTER 16:

THE NEXT TIME I ASK FOR $1000, JUST GIVE ME A VEGGIE BURGER INSTEAD!

Sometimes when we try to communicate, everything goes wrong and we don't understand why. Perhaps we're more prone to argue than usual, or maybe we're having trouble focusing or listening. Once you realize this is happening, take a moment to connect with yourself. Take a break from the conversation to assess your physical and emotional state. Is there something going on that's interfering and making things difficult?

Kyeli's Story: The Best Veggie Burger Ever!

Pace and I were talking about money. The subject was often stressful because we have opposing money issues and we tend to accidentally tread on each other's landmines. This particular time, we had recently merged our separate bank accounts to a joint account, which we were mostly happy about doing. We'd done the merge mid-month and this caused some problems. A few days before we merged our accounts, Pace invested $10,000 out of her bank accounts: $9000 out of savings and $1000 out of checking. We then merged the accounts. On the first of the new month, we were short that same $1000 for various bills. We were hit with a slew of overdraft fees and had to scramble to cover rent.

The resulting discussion got heated. Pace felt frustrated and was afraid of losing her money. I felt frustrated too, trying to get her to understand that the $1000 she'd invested from her checking account had been the money we needed, because it would have been her share of our bills had we not merged. She got angry, I got upset, and we wound up yelling at each other.

Eventually, we decided to take a break, a time-out for resting and remembering that we were trying to solve a common problem and could work together instead of fighting each other. We decided to eat veggie burgers for dinner.

Pace took one bite, *one bite*, shook her head, and said, "I am being greedy and selfish. That money was totally ours, I accidentally invested too much, and I will happily take care of the mess we're in." I looked at her agog, and she grinned that bright, beautiful smile and said, *"The next time I ask for $1000, just give me a veggie burger instead!"*

Pace's problem wasn't actually anger, it was hunger. She used to get unfocused, zoned-out, and prickly when she was hungry, but she wouldn't realize it until she snapped at Kyeli. This is another time when it's good to remember that *we are made of meat.* We can't think or communicate clearly when our bodies are distracted by physical needs; this is a normal consequence of having a human body.

There are several states that affect us negatively, any of which can knock us out of whack and make successful communication more difficult. Here are some of the more common ones:

hungry

sleepy

exhausted

in pain (e.g. headache, cramps, sprains)

drugged (e.g. drunk, on pain medication)

uncomfortable (physically or emotionally)

sexually frustrated

angry

distracted

triggered

When you find that you're no longer in a good place to communicate, find a good place to pause the conversation until your situation can be remedied. If you're hungry, eat. If you're sleepy or exhausted, ease the conversation to a good stopping place (or at least a good place to pause) so you can get some rest.

Anger is trickier to handle. If you or your partner feels angry, it can be difficult to communicate well. Simply pausing to take a break doesn't always work, because walking away from an angry person can make them more angry. We've found that it's best to work through the anger first before continuing to discuss the original issues. Calm down or help calm your partner down as best you can, talk through the anger, or find a different method that works. Pause to deal with the anger rather than pausing to wait for it to go away.

Kyeli's Story:

Care and Feeding of the Wild Pace

With Pace, I found that I would notice her hunger before she would. I became good at noticing it, in fact, so I took it upon myself to check with her and see if I could provide her with food. This can be tricky, especially if your loved one is touchy when hungry. I got snapped at quite often until Pace learned to notice her mood on her own.

I discovered that, if I shifted the focus to myself, I could check with her in an inoffensive manner. I would approach her with, "Hey, I'm feeling hungry. How are you? Can we eat something?" Naturally, if I wasn't hungry, I'd find some other way, because otherwise I'd be lying, but I found that making it about me instead of her made it much more likely to resolve the issue instead of further upsetting her.

As for me, it's difficult for me to get a good night's sleep if I'm upset. There have been many nights when we've stayed up until dawn discussing difficult things because I can't unwind with my emotions in upheaval. Pace has problems with this because when she gets sleepy, she has an incredibly difficult time staying focused or awake. We've dealt with this by stopping before she gets too sleepy, and making time for cuddling and reassurance before we actually fall asleep. This often helps, but not always, and when it doesn't, I'll get up and entertain myself for a little while until I'm calm enough to sleep.

An easy way to remember when to pause communication is with *H.A.L.T.: Hungry, Angry, Loopy, Tired.*[1] If you're feeling hungry, angry, loopy, or tired, consider postponing communication until your situation improves. It's tough enough to communicate when our bodies are getting everything they need and are in a good state. If we don't have enough food, if our emotions are too intense to allow us to think about anything else, if we're drugged, if we're sleepy, or if we're otherwise encumbered, it will make communication even more challenging.

In summary, communication becomes more difficult when you have physical or emotional factors affecting your state of well-being. Pay attention to how you and your partner are doing. If you notice a reason to H.A.L.T., pause the conversation and get back to a state of well-being before continuing.

---

1   We learned this from 12-step programs like Alcoholics Anonymous. Originally, the L stood for "lonely," which is spot-on for addiction recovery, but "loopy" (by which we mean "in an altered mental state, for example on pain medication") is more relevant to communication.

Chapter 17:

We're on the same team

Have you ever started a conversation with a friend and had it turn into an argument? Have you ever tried to help someone solve a problem and ended up in a fight? We tend to get defensive, even when we're not really being threatened — even when *we're on the same team*. When we notice this happening in our lives, we remind ourselves out loud: "We're on the same team." This simple phrase can single-handedly turn a potential conflict into a helpful conversation.

Kyeli's Story: Defuse Me Like a Bomb

The simple phrase "We're on the same team" can bring me up out of anger or hurt feelings. It doesn't magically make everything better, but it does remind me that Pace isn't out to get me, isn't trying to hurt me, and hasn't maliciously pushed my emotional buttons. It sounds ridiculous, but we tend to feel victimized when we've just been hurt by something our partner has done or said, no matter how close we are or how much trust we share. It helps me a lot to hear her remind me that she's on my team. It often moves me from a defensive position to one where I'm much more able to communicate and be comforted.

One night, we discussed our feelings about an ex-friend who had tried to re-establish communication with us. This person had deeply hurt me before severing all ties a few months back and I was not feeling open or accepting of her. Pace felt differently and we were working through many issues to get at the roots of how we felt. Through the course of the conversation, I started to feel like she wasn't on my team anymore. I felt it was her vs. me and that she was trying to rationalize my feelings. I started snapping at her, getting defensive, and feeling hurt. Communication slowed to a crawl.

Eventually, I figured out what was happening and I was able to tell her, "Right now, it doesn't feel like we're on the same team! I feel like you're against me!"

We stopped the conversation and took some time out. She hugged me (reconnecting through physical contact is a great way to remember you love the person you're upset with) and reminded me that we wanted the same outcome: we wanted to come to a decision *together* about how to handle this situation to make both of us happy. We were, as usual, on the same team. Having that connection re-established, I was able to calm down significantly and go back to our original conversation.

Sometimes, it feels like you and your partner aren't on the same team, even when you know you are. If you're lost in the throes of emotion during a heated conversation, it's easy to lose sight of your common goals. You may feel like you oppose your partner or that your partner opposes you. These are the times when taking a short break to say out loud, "We're on the same team here; we want the same thing and we care about each other" is important. It helps you remember that it's not you versus your partner, it's you and your partner on the same team, working together against the problem.

Pace's Story: Design vs. Design — Fight!

At work, I discussed the design of an upcoming project with a teammate. I came up with my idea for the design and he came up with his. We argued about the pros and cons of the two different approaches for quite some time and we didn't really get anywhere. We had become attached to our ideas and had accidentally gotten into a confrontation, as if the two of us were fighting against each other. But it wasn't true; there was no need for us to fight. We both wanted to accomplish the same goal; we both wanted to solve the same problem. "We're on the same team," I reminded him (and myself!). Once we remembered that we were on the same team, the conversation changed from a stressful confrontation into a positive, useful discussion. We considered the ideas on their own merits rather than on our attachments to them. By doing this, we made a good decision and moved forward with it — together.

"We're on the same team" works in any situation where people share a common goal. Saying it out loud can remind everyone involved that they want to work together to achieve a goal, rather than battling it out amongst one another. Try it! Say these words out loud the next time you feel that someone is forgetting that you're on the same team with them. It has worked wonders for us and we hope it will be equally wonderful for you.

CHAPTER 18:

COMING TO TERMS

Mary and Kathi's Example:

A Few Sandwiches

Mary: "I'm hungry. What is there to eat?"

Kathi: "There were a few sandwiches left over from dinner last night. I put them in the fridge."

Mary: "I can't find them. I only ate three this afternoon. Where are the rest?"

Kathi: "Oh, I think that's about all there were, three or so."

Mary: "I thought you said there were a few!"

Kathi: "Yeah, you know, a few, three or so."

Mary: "What?! Everyone knows 'a few' means at least five or six. Now what am I supposed to eat?"

People have different definitions of words. In fact, everyone speaks their own unique dialect of their language. Linguists call this idiosyncratic dialect an *idiolect* and everyone's is different. What this boils down to is that everyone is speaking a different language, all the time. We don't usually notice we're speaking different languages. The differences are so subtle that we think we have communicated successfully. However, if two people have different definitions for a word in their two separate idiolects, they may misunderstand each other without even realizing that a misunderstanding has occurred.

Mary and Kathi's story illustrates a simple case of two people having different definitions for the same phrase. They quickly notice the difference. They each made the usual error in assuming that the other person's definition was the same as theirs. Now what do they do about it?

As we've learned, it might be best to delay talking about it until they've eaten. After that, it's time for Mary and Kathi to *come to terms*. There are three ways that they can come to terms:

1. Mary can choose to adopt Kathi's definition.

2. Kathi can choose to adopt Mary's definition.

3. Each person can choose to acknowledge the other person's definition and attempt to keep it in mind during future conversations.

Which of these three options is best? If your definition is entirely idiosyncratic, and it seems like everyone else you communicate with uses the other definition, then you may wish to come to terms by adopting the more widely used definition. Doing this will help others understand you better. Consulting a dictionary can be helpful, but is not always representative of how a term is actually used. It's a good source for the literal definition of a word, but it doesn't convey the feel or tone of a word very well. Furthermore, the people with whom you frequently communicate may use the word differently than the dictionary definition. Choose your words based on what you feel will help you communicate most effectively. The dictionary is your tool, not your boss.

The dictionary does not contain the one right way to use a word. There *is* no one right way to use a word. Languages evolve and specialize, regardless of what is written in dictionaries. If one person's definition happens to match the dictionary definition, that does not make that person right and the other person wrong. In the above example, Mary said, "Everyone knows 'a few' means at least five or six." The phrase "everyone knows" is an attacking phrase, implying that not only are Mary and Kathi on opposite teams, but that "everyone" else is on Mary's team. She was attempting to make herself feel right and Kathi feel wrong and outnumbered. Mary could have phrased that more positively and cooperatively by saying, "Hmm, I define 'a few' to mean at least five or six. I guess you and I have different definitions of 'a few'. Let's talk about that after we've eaten, okay?"

Here are some terms that many people define in vastly differing ways. We've found that it's well worth the time spent having conversations about our different definitions of these, *before* they cause problems.

love

sex

friend

boyfriend / girlfriend

date / dating

relationship

degree words, like "very", "quite", "a little", "a lot", especially when pertaining to feelings

sure

okay

time degree words, like "soon" and "ASAP"

high priority

support

assume

God and other religious terms

Kyeli's Story: Define Your Date

The issue of differing definitions came up for us most dramatically around the word "date."

Pace was romantically interested in a friend of ours, and this friend was also romantically interested in Pace. The two of them wanted to go to dinner alone every couple of weeks or so. This sparked many conversations between Pace and me. I had strong emotional reactions to Pace's desire to go out with this friend, because she and I had agreed that we would not date other people and I felt Pace was violating that agreement. I insisted that it felt like Pace and our friend were "dating." Pace insisted that the romantic interest was irrelevant, she did not intend to act on it, and that they were "just two friends occasionally going out to dinner."

I pointed out that they were "just two friends" with mutual romantic interest, going out to dinner *alone,* and that if I wanted to go along, I would not be welcome. Pace agreed that this was true and I argued that that made it a date.

I continued to insist they were dating, Pace continued to insist they were not. We butted heads until we realized that at the foundation of all of these problems lay a difference in our definitions of the word "date." According to my definition, Pace was dating her friend, but according to her definition, she wasn't.

All this conflict had been due to a misunderstanding of what the word "date" meant to each of us.

Once we understood that we were defining "date" differently, we were able to stop arguing about definitions and start working together to resolve the underlying issues about the boundaries of our relationship. We reworked our agreement to be more precise about what "date" meant, and in the process we came a little closer to speaking each other's language and a *lot* closer to understanding each other better.

Degree terms (as listed above) can be especially tricky. Our brains sometimes take liberties with degree words and interpret them as larger or smaller than they were actually intended. For example, let's say that Pace feels insecure about her cooking. Pace asks what Kyeli thought of dinner and she replies, "It was yummy, it was just a little overdone." What Pace hears is "It was overdone," completely missing the "just a little." As a result, her insecurity reinforces itself and she gets upset.

It's possible to come to terms with degree words like any other words, but we've found it useful to treat them specially, because of their tendency to be misconstrued. We use a scale from -10 to +10, with -10 being incredibly horrible, 0 being neutral, and +10 being incredibly wonderful. Simply having a scale doesn't solve anything, because numbers are still words and can have vastly different meanings to each of us. So we came to terms on several of the numbers, talking about how good or bad different experiences were for us and agreeing on a shared scale. Now we can accurately compare our preferences. We talk about what we want to do, and when we want different things, we ask, "How much do you want that?" "Oh, about a +4. How would you feel if we did this instead?" "Actually, that would be about a -6 for me." Of course, it doesn't work unless you're honest, but that's true for everything we talk about in this book.

Probability and certainty words are also degree words:

> necessarily
>
> probably
>
> possibly
>
> maybe
>
> absolutely
>
> certainly

Watch out for sneaky brain tricks and the tendency to be misconstrued again! We've come across many examples: "I'll probably be there" can be heard as "I'll be there," "That isn't necessarily what I would have done" can be heard as "That isn't what I would have done," and so on. We like to use numbers for probability and certainty words too, but we use a percentage scale instead of a -10 to +10 scale, for example, "I'm 80% sure I'll be able to make it that night," or "I'm 99% certain that what I told you was correct."

For those of our readers who are polyamorous[1], here are some poly-specific words and phrases that are often defined differently by different people:

---

[1] Polyamory is the practice of having multiple romantic relationships at the same time, openly and honestly. *Polyamory: The New Love Without Limits* by Deborah Anapol is a good introduction to polyamory, as is the website www.lovemore.com.

polyamory

primary

secondary

tertiary

polyfidelity

long-distance relationship

Assuming that other people's definitions (or connotations) of words are the same as yours is a common case of the usual error. Many arguments and debates, especially on the internet, end up boiling down to a difference in definitions. We've listed some trouble words that have come up in our experience, but we've probably made the usual error too; your trouble words may be different. In any case, when you notice a miscommunication, keep in mind that it might be due to a difference in definitions, and see if you can come to terms.

CHAPTER 19:

META-COMMUNICATION

Meta-communication is communication about communication. When communication isn't working, you can use meta-communication to help you figure out why and to make things better in the future. Many of the techniques we talk about are meta-communication in a broad sense, but in this chapter we'll talk about a particular kind of meta-communication: conversations you can have once to make lots of future conversations better.

What if someone often uses a particular word or phrase that sparks an unhelpfully defensive reaction in you? Meta-communication can help: bring it up a single time so you don't continue tripping over it again and again. What if a particular kind of misunderstanding arises over and over again? Meta-communication can help: bring it up once to talk about how to avoid the misunderstanding in the future or how to deal with it more gracefully when it does happen.

Pace's Story: Learning to Emote

Kyeli and I used to have lots of miscommunications because I'm still learning to emote: to express my emotions nonverbally. She would often perceive my lack of facial expression as me feeling distant or cold, when on my end I was simply forgetting or neglecting to emote. We had some meta-communication about this; we talked about this issue, including some helpful examples from recent conversations. Kyeli talked about her perceptions and feelings. I talked about why emoting is difficult for me given how I was raised. We came to a better understanding of each other, and since then, every time this has happened it's been less of a problem.

What if a contentious topic arises frequently and there's no easy solution? Meta-communication can help to figure out boundaries. If the topic can be postponed or only discussed at specific times, then you can limit or reduce the unpleasantness. On the other hand, if it's not something that can be postponed or ignored, then the only way out is through.

Pace's Story: Meta-Money

Money used to be a problematic issue for us. We argued about it once or twice a week. It stressed us out and I wanted to make it better, so I asked for some meta-communication. We talked about how we could reduce the frequency or unpleasantness of the money conversations. After talking about it for a while, we agreed to stick to our budget during the month and let non-urgent money conversations wait until the end of the month, when we balance the monthly budget. This works much better for us. We still have a stressful conversation once a month, but that's a vast improvement over having it happen all the time.

Having one big stressful conversation can feel daunting and scary, but in the long run it's usually better than having lots of little stressful conversations more frequently.

Meta-communication can also be used to pause a conversation in order to talk about an important issue that might be blocking progress on the main conversation. If progress in a conversation is slow or difficult, consider using meta-communication to figure out why.

Kyeli's Story: A Tangent of Reconnection

One night, we were having an intense discussion. I got upset and lost in the emotions I was feeling. Pace offered me a hug, but I said I was not in a place to be hugged right then.

She said she wanted to help me feel better before we continued the original discussion, so we postponed everything to talk about how hurt and conflicted I was feeling. I talked a while, had a good cry, and worked it out until I felt more clear. Then we hugged (several times), and settled back into the original conversation.

It was important to me that we engaged in this form of meta-communication. If we hadn't taken time out to reconnect and reassure each other that

we're on the same team, the conversation would have
only become worse and I would have gotten more
and more upset.

In this story, we stopped our initial conversation to have an
important meta-conversation about reconnecting and being on
the same team. When we felt resolved with the meta-conversation, we returned to the initial conversation.

It can help to have a meta-conversation if you find yourself
becoming upset, getting lost in your emotions, or if the original
conversation gets stuck for some other reason. Meta-communi-
cate to find solutions to recurring problems, to make frequent
stresses less frequent or less stressful, and to unblock progress
on a stuck conversation.

CHAPTER 20:

MEMORY

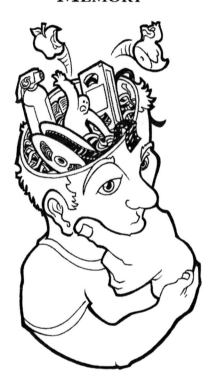

We like to think that we have a single memory, an auto-biographical history of ourselves stretching backwards into our past, from the present back to when we were very young. We understand that there are gaps and that it gets more vague the further back we go, but we still have the impression of a single fairly consistent record of time. We rarely question its accuracy. If we say, "He was there. I remember seeing him,"

others will likely believe us. We believe that our eyes and ears are like video cameras, relaying sights and sounds to our brain, which records everything for later use like a mental VCR.

Memory isn't like that at all. In truth, we have a collection of fragments and familiarities. We process only a fraction of the information our senses take in, and far less makes it into our long-term memory. Our long-term memory fades over time, leaving islands of memory in a sea of haze. What's more, even those islands may be difficult to recall. Many of our memories lie dormant, requiring specific reminders to "jog our memories" and bring them to the surface.

Despite these facts, we tend to feel deeply and viscerally that our memories are reliable and truthful sources of knowledge about the past. We base our attitudes and opinions on our memories; we hinge our entire worldviews on them. How do we maintain the illusion that memory is reliable? The answer, though it might be difficult to believe, is that we fill in the gaps by *making stuff up*. We paste our current opinions onto the memories of the past. We fill holes in memories with explanations that make sense to us. We reinvent the past in the image of the present.

Memory is blurry; it has far less detail than the original perceptions it comes from. Many people store perceptual memories *verbally*, turning a scene remembered several times into a game of telephone played with one's own mind.

Kyeli's Story: A Bear at the Door

When I was little, my family went on a trip to Colorado. During the entire drive, my dad told us stories about bears. He told us how careful we had to be when outside, how dangerous the bears were, how many of them there were, and how they would eat kids who fought with their parents (hah!). Our first night in the hotel, my mom was in the bathroom bathing my little brother. My dad went to get ice from the ice machine. I was in my nightgown, jumping on the beds.

There was a knock at our hotel door. I jumped down, and being a helpful kid, asked, "Who is it?"

There commenced a growling and scratching at the door, louder and more fierce than anything I'd ever heard in my life. A bear! I just knew it was a bear! I started screaming incoherently. My mother raced out of the bathroom to see why I was screaming my fool head off. I ran into the bathroom, closed and locked the door, and told my brother we were going to be eaten by a bear. He, too, started screaming.

My mother let my father back into the room and he came in sheepishly and apologetically. It took the two of them a good hour to calm us down enough to convince me to unlock the bathroom door and let them in.

This all happened when I was six.

I no longer have any real memory of this event, but growing up, I heard the story from my parents enough to have it blazed into my memory. I've told it hundreds of times myself; I even turned it into a short story and won an award for it. But truth be told, it's all a story to me now.

Memory is inherently biased. We don't record the actual facts or perceptions of what we experience; we record our *interpretation* of those perceptions. For example, if we see a cloud, and we interpret it to be shaped like a duck, we will remember "duck-shaped cloud" rather than recording an image of the cloud seen by our eyes. When we later recall the cloud, we will remember it as more duck-shaped than it actually was. This interpretation happens automatically, entirely outside of our conscious mind, and involves such filters as our worldview, our frame of mind, and our mood. This unconscious interpretation occurs *before memories are stored.* Not only are our memories modified after the fact, they are unreliable from the get-go.

Memories are more extreme than reality. As a rule, we tend to remember colors as being brighter or deeper, slow speeds as being slower, fast speeds as being faster, large things as being larger, small things as being smaller, and duck-shaped things as being duckier. Even without purposeful exaggeration, stories like "The fish was *this big!*" end up bigger than the truth.

Memory changes with the telling. The more often a memory is recounted, the more distorted it becomes. Each telling rewrites the event, allowing more errors of interpretation to creep in. Quantities become more extreme, events and situations change to better fit into our current opinions of the people and situations involved, and present influences, attitudes, and concepts are written into the past.

A striking example of the fallacy of memory involves a man named Donald Thompson and the most ironic arrest of all time. Thompson, a psychologist doing research into the reliability of eyewitness memory, was brought in for a lineup and positively identified by a rape victim as the man who had raped her. It was later revealed that Thompson had in fact been far away at the time, on live television, in a panel discussion about the unreliability of memory. Despite this, the woman continued to swear under oath that she firmly remembered him as the culprit. Eventually the truth was revealed: the victim's television had been turned on to that very program during the crime, and the actual rapist had been wearing similar clothes. This was all it took to fabricate a clear and intense memory of Thompson as the criminal.[1]

Kyeli's Story: Tom and Flat Cat

My brother and I are only four years apart. We grew up in the same houses with the same parents, usually

[1]   The source for this example is Daniel Schacter's book *Searching for Memory*, page 114.

going to the same schools. We grew up around the same cousins and the same grandparents. We even occasionally had overlapping friends.

If you ask him about our relationship as children, he'll tell you we mostly got along. In his memory, we were friends for the majority of our lives.

If you ask me, you'll get a totally different answer! In my memory, we were usually enemies. We fought and argued, punched and kicked and yelled at each other all the time. Our memories are so radically different, I often wonder how we lived the same life for so long!

We had two cats when we were little: Tom and Flat Cat. In my memory, Tom was my cat. I remember this quite clearly; he was the sweetest cat I've ever had. He let me put doll clothes on him and carry him around like a baby. Flat Cat, a grouchy pudge of surly gray fur, was my brother's cat. Again, my memory is crystal clear on this. However, in my brother's memory, the cats were reversed: Tom was his and Flat Cat was mine. To explain the behavior of Tom, my brother will tell you that Tom was so tolerant it didn't matter who he belonged to.

We're each *entirely certain* of entirely opposite memories!

We make the usual error every time we remember something. Not only are we living with different perceptions, different points of view, different personality types, and different communication styles, we each have our own separate memories — basically our own separate *worlds*. Quite literally, what happened for you and what happened for someone else can seem totally different, even when a video camera would tell us that the situation was the same. What's more, unless things have been recorded on film or other objective evidence exists, neither memory can justly be treated as more real than the other.

This sounds like a desperate and confusing situation. What can we do about it? Improving the reliability of our memory isn't an effective solution because memory by its very nature will always be biased and subjective. If you need an objective account, write it down! If you have an important meeting at work, write down the outcome and email it to everyone involved to make sure everyone has the same understanding. This guards against the fallibility of memory and is also a form of reflection. If you have an important conversation, write down a summary and the outcome. If you keep a journal, use it. That way, if you can't remember what was said or how you were feeling about a particular event in the past, you can look it up.

These suggestions can help for many cases, but there will always be things that are unwritten and unrecorded. In those cases, there is no way to find out the objective truth. This may feel scary, but people seem to get by pretty well despite this. We feel strongly attached to our memories — we feel that they're the *truth* — but arguing about differing memories is usually pointless and rarely leads to a helpful resolution of an argument. When a conflict arises about something in the past, we often find ourselves arguing, attempting to find who has the "best" memory, arguing over our different recollections of what "actually" happened. Instead of arguing, we can remember that our memories are *not* accurate recordings of the truth, and neither are anyone else's. Remembering this frees you to explore other options. Regardless of what happened in the past, your feelings in the present are still valid and important, and *that's* something that you can talk about constructively. When talking about past events, use "I" statements. When you have the urge to say, "You're wrong, what really happened was this," instead say, "My memory is different. The way I remember it is this." Letting go of the past to focus on the present can be hard, but it's the best way we've found to turn a memory-related conflict into constructive communication.

Chapter 21:

Trust your future self

People worry about a wide variety of things, some silly, some serious. We worry about our job security, we worry about our health, we worry about our reputations. Most of the things we worry about are at least partially out of our control. This chapter is about the other cases: cases when the problem is completely *within* our control!

The most obvious case of worrying about something entirely within our control is worrying about our own feelings or desires.

We worry that our feelings will change and that we won't want the same things we do now. The weight of these worries can paralyze us, stunning us into indecision and stagnation. If this happens to you, you can *trust your future self.*

Pace's Story: Trusting My Future Self

Kyeli and I were once worried that we might fall out of love with each other. We were worried that our feelings might eventually change. We worried about this for a while, but through much discussion eventually chose to *trust our future selves.* If our feelings change in the future, then we'll figure out how we feel and what we want at that time, and we'll do what we most want to do. If what we want is to stay together, then we *will* stay together. If what we want is to no longer stay together, then there's *still* no sense worrying about it now, because we'd just be worrying about what our future selves want to do. If we each want different things, then there's no sense worrying about that either — I very much want Kyeli to be happy, so if her feelings eventually change, my future self would want to respect that. No one but us has any say over our relationship; it's entirely within our control. What a silly thing to worry about!

This can be a difficult concept, but it's important and can save you quite a lot of needless worry. People spend a huge amount of time and energy worrying over decisions that, in the long run, won't be so dramatically important a few years, weeks, or even days down the road. Once you learn to trust your future self, you may find that your energy and time are better spent *doing* things instead of *worrying* about doing them.

Kyeli's Story:

It's My Party, and I'll Go If I Want To!

We used to spend lots of time and energy worrying whenever there was a social event on our calendar. We worried about going or not going. We worried about whether we'd enjoy ourselves if we went. We worried about whether we'd regret it if we stayed home. We spent lots of time and effort worrying about whether going would be worth the time and effort. Now, we know to trust our future selves in all aspects. If we choose to go and wind up having a lousy time, we can leave and come home (it's not as hard or as awkward as we feared!). If we stay home and start feeling regretful, we can go late. We now spend our time and energy on enjoying ourselves no matter what we choose, rather than spending it on worrying about what to choose, because our choices are entirely under our control!

Keep an eye out for situations where you're worrying about something that's actually completely under your control. There are probably more of them than you imagine! A frequent tip-off to this type of situation is worrying about what you might or might not want in the future. Save yourself from this unnecessary stress and worry. Trust your future self.

CHAPTER 22:

GIVING PERMISSION TO DISAPPOINT

The myth of the perfect romantic relationship has inflicted a lot of damage. We see it primarily in its most common manifestation: the myth of "one true love." It tells us to spend our early lives looking and waiting for "the one." We hear it in movies all the time: "Could she be the one?" or "I've finally found Mr. Right!" The myth says that "the one" will drop into your life and be perfect for you. The two of you will fit together like puzzle pieces and live happily ever after. All your problems will be solved now that you and your soul mate have finally found each other, because you're perfect for each other.

This is utter nonsense! People are not anything like puzzle pieces. We each have rough, irregular edges, and even the most compatible friends or partners in the world won't fit seamlessly. There will be conflict, difficulty, and friction throughout the entire duration of even the healthiest relationships.

That's not a bad thing. It's part of what's wonderful about relationships. There's always something to understand more clearly, rough edges to smooth out, problems to solve, and adventures to share.

In any relationship there will be times when someone feels disappointed or hurt by someone else's action, inaction, or words. When this happens, we have a choice of how to deal with it: we can continue to insist that it's just not supposed to happen, or we can actively allow for it in our lives. We can *give permission to disappoint each other.*

This works for relationships of all types. How amazing would it be if your boss recognized the fact that there was going to be some friction in your working relationship, and explicitly gave you permission to disappoint him? Giving permission to disappoint works for any relationship where the people involved are on the same team and occasionally even when you're not.

When we disappoint each other, we lose our ability to solve the problem at hand because we get caught up in how we feel about the disappointment. We may feel ashamed to disappoint our partner or afraid of admitting our own limitations and needs. Or, if we've been disappointed, we may feel conflict between our perfect concept of our partner (stemming from the perfection myth) and the reality of the disappointment. We may paint the other person as somehow lacking because they didn't live up to our mythical expectations.

With all those distractions, it's a wonder we manage to solve any problems at all! If instead we give each other permission to disappoint, we can move beyond the distracting issues and deal with what's really going on. Giving permission to disappoint takes the sting from it, and helps us focus on the actual cause of the disappointment.

Here's a suggestion: get together with one person you trust and explicitly give them permission to disappoint you. If you feel they would be open to it, ask if they wish to give you permission to disappoint them as well. Imagine how that would feel if they accepted. How would that change your future interactions with them? How would it feel the next time you let them down? If it works well, give it a try with others too!

Pace's Story: Playing Video Games

A few years ago, a situation that often came up in my day-to-day life was that I would feel like playing video games but Sera (my ex) would prefer to do something together. Whenever I chose to play video games, I felt like I was disappointing Sera with my choice, and I felt like *that wasn't okay*. After this situation occurred many times, and I built up a lot of stress and worry about it, we had some good meta-communication. During the meta-conversation, Sera gave me permission to disappoint her. It was incredible! I never even considered the possibility that this was something for which permission could be given! I never even considered the possibility that it was okay to disappoint *anyone!* It was amazing!

A few days later, I was playing a video game for a long time, and Sera got impatient and frustrated. At first, I reacted with dismay that I had disappointed her. But then I remembered that it was okay — she had given me permission! After that, instead of flipping out about me disappointing her, we had a fruitful conversation about how we could each get what we need.

Giving permission to disappoint

You can give yourself permission to disappoint others, too! We're often hard on ourselves when we disappoint people, especially those we care about. We feel like it's not okay, like we're bad, like we're failures for disappointing them, but it *is* okay, as long as we're being genuine. (Don't, however, take this too far and give yourself permission to be cruel.) Everyone disappoints others sometimes, everyone makes mistakes, and feeling bad about it isn't going to do you — or them — any good. Giving yourself permission to disappoint is giving yourself permission to be human, to be flawed, and to be yourself.

PART IV:
CONFLICT RESOLUTION

CHAPTER 23:

THE ONLY WAY OUT IS THROUGH

Communication is rewarding, but difficult. It takes effort to figure out your own communication style and to figure out how it differs from the communication styles of those around you. It takes work to identify and hold your boundaries and to respect others'. We feel at odds with those closest to us, even when they're on our side. We feel trapped in the messes we create.

Sometimes, we get overwhelmed with all this and we want to *stop*. We want to stop talking, stop having problems, stop everything! Can't we take a break? Can't we just go a few *days* without communicating about anything important?

Kyeli's Story: Scream Real Loud!

In autumn of 2005, Pace and I went through many intense relationship discussions in preparation for our wedding. After several weeks of this, Pace got frustrated and angrily said, "Can't we just go one month with no hard discussions? Or with no discussions about relationships at all?!"

I stubbornly clammed up and an entire month passed. Tension occasionally mounted, but I never spoke to Pace about anything significant. I would often talk to many of my close friends to vent my feelings, but utterly refused to discuss anything with Pace. It felt so frustrating I wanted to scream! Pace eventually forgot about her request, but I didn't, and I went well out of my way to avoid any kind of communication revolving around our relationship.

Finally, the eve before our wedding, Pace asked if we could talk to be sure we were still on the same page. As it'd been exactly a month, I agreed. We talked for five hours and the joy we felt at the end was palpable! We'd been feeling so disconnected, so removed from each other. We wound up crying and holding each other while we talked... and when we finally reached the end and had trailed off, cuddling and relaxing, Pace asked why we'd gone so long without talking. I reminded her of her request and Pace said, "What? That was stupid! If I ever ask for that again, just... I don't know... do something drastic that'll remind me what a doofus I felt like tonight!"

"Scream?" I suggested, fluttering my eyelashes at her.

"Sure. Scream real loud. That'll do it."

Fast forward many months... Once again, we went through a period of many intense relationship discussions. After many days of this, Pace got frustrated and asked, "Can't we just go one--"

I took a deep breath and screamed at the top of my lungs. I screamed for so long I nearly passed out.

When I finally stopped, she looked at me agog, completely baffled as to why I could possibly be screaming bloody murder in response to her simple question.

"Well," I said, "you asked for it."

A moment of thought passed, then Pace remembered, brightened, and laughed a big, hearty laugh. "Thanks!" she said. We hugged and went on to have many more excellent conversations.

Sometimes we need a break from communicating about sensitive subjects. If you're feeling burned out on a particular issue, a hiatus can be a good thing. The problem lies in forcing a break for too long a period of time. One of the big dangers of a ceasefire in communication is *stewing*. If you have a problem and don't discuss it for a long period of time, it can lead to much bigger problems.

Kyeli's Story: Richard's Email Stew

Right after I moved to Dallas, I worked for several months for Richard, a local entrepreneur. At one point, Richard created a new email address for me and neglected to inform me. Many weeks later, things came to a head. He said he had been sending me emails and, from his perspective, I had completely ignored them. When we finally talked, we discovered that I didn't even know this email address existed and I hadn't been getting the emails he thought I was ignoring.

Sadly, this was realized too late. The weeks of stewing had irreparably tarnished his opinion of me. The damage had already been done and we were no longer able to work together comfortably. If instead of stewing, he had talked to me when he first felt ignored, we might have been able to salvage our business relationship.

The only way out is through. The only way out from inside a problem is to get through it — to talk and work it through, to communicate, listen, and work together with your partner to get your relationship through the problem and to a happier place. This is the case nearly every time a problem happens; talking it through is the way to a peaceful, secure relationship. We often feel a lot of resistance to having these big conversations, but it's better to get through them rather than trying to delay or avoid them.

Sometimes you may find that the only way out is to end a relationship, and that's okay. It's most often the case that a relationship, business or personal, can be repaired through communication (far more often than we're led to believe), but occasionally a relationship cannot be repaired and must be ended. That was what happened in Kyeli's example from her job above. By the time real communication occurred, the damage to their trust was too great to be worked through. It is sad when that happens, but in those cases, letting go and moving forward is a valid option.

When you wish to maintain a healthy, happy, and secure relationship, however — the only way out is through.

CHAPTER 24:

THE WILLIAM JAMES ZONE

*"Actually, I'm still feeling upset. Remember, I
have a bigger William James than you."*

All the clear communication you've been learning can be completely muddied if you don't communicate clearly with yourself. Part of self-communication is paying attention to your emotions and your body when you get angry. This helps stop your anger from getting out of control and muddying everything up.

When you get angry, your brain sends out signals to your body. Your adrenaline pumps and your body releases hormones.

Anger prods your body, saying, "Get ready to act!" Anger is an emotion, but it's also a physical state. Once that adrenaline starts pumping, your *body* becomes angry. Even if the cause of the emotional anger goes away, the physical anger is still there, and it starts a feedback loop. Your brain asks your body, "How are we doing?" Your body replies, "We're really angry!" Your brain reacts by becoming emotionally angry in response to the physical anger, causing your brain to send out anger signals to your body again, and the feedback loop continues.

Brains are surprisingly good at inventing reasons for being angry, even if the original reason has gone away and the only real remaining cause is the adrenaline in the bloodstream. It can be *physically impossible* to let go of anger until your body has settled down. The rate at which your body returns to its baseline non-angry state varies from person to person. Being in this state of reinforced physical anger is what we call the *William James zone*, and how long it takes you to get out of that zone is your "William James threshold." The philosopher William James predicted this effect long before the science of biology was able to confirm it,[1] which is why we named this effect after him. The stereotype is that women take longer to cool down from anger than men do, but every person's William James threshold will depend on circumstance, upbringing, mood, and multiple other factors. It's best to avoid making assumptions and instead learn to deal with people as individuals.

Jane and Joe's Example:

Shattering the Stereotype

Jane and Joe are having a huge argument. They yell at each other for a long time, both upset and neither communicating in a useful or effective manner. After

---

1   William James predicted this effect in 1884 in his article *What is an Emotion?* which was published in volume 9 of the journal *Mind*, on pages 188-205.

a while, they stop yelling. Jane sincerely apologizes for her thoughtlessness and Joe thanks her. They kiss. Jane goes into the living room, plops down on the sofa, and turns on the television. Meanwhile, Joe is still in the kitchen and still upset. He needs another outlet for his anger, so he calls his friend and spends half an hour on the phone, complaining about Jane's thoughtless behavior, her rudeness, and the argument they just had, as well as every argument he can remember in their entire history, and hey, she didn't even hang the laundry this morning!

Jane's in the living room, totally clueless that Joe's still upset. She is out of her William James zone. She feels resolved and content, and isn't even thinking about the argument anymore.

Joe, in the kitchen, is still in his William James zone. He's gotten resolution for the most recent argument, but his body is still full of anger, so when his brain checks, he gets the "we're still angry" response, and continues constructing reasons to hold on to the anger. Since he's still in the zone, and his feedback loop is still looping, he hangs up the phone and heads into the living room to pick another fight with Jane.

Jane's been watching TV this whole time, has no idea Joe is still mad, and is flabbergasted when Joe starts yelling at her.

All of this is useful to know, but what does it have to do with communication and problem solving? The answer is this: if you're aware of the difference between emotional anger and physical anger, some situations become much easier to handle. For instance, if you know that the person with whom you're communicating has a long William James threshold, when they get angry you can ask for some time to cool down before continuing the conversation. It might be helpful to take a break, to go outside for a few minutes and take a walk, or to be in separate rooms for a while. If anyone involved in the conflict is experiencing physical anger, it will be especially difficult to communicate successfully. This is why it's often better to wait it out. Cool-down time is a good thing to negotiate before anyone gets upset so that you can ask for it in the moment in a way that won't cause tempers to flare up even higher.

Being aware of the William James zone can also help you be more understanding of other people's anger. If you realize that your partner is angry because of something going on in their body rather than because of anything you did, it can help put their angry outburst into perspective. A deeper understanding of what's actually going on allows you to react with more compassion.

Furthermore, being able to realize when *you* are in the William James zone can help you overcome your physical anger. If you remember that sometimes anger can be purely physical, and that your brain invents random reasons to explain it, you can temper yourself before you turn that physical anger into destructive words or actions.

Kyeli's Story: In the Zone

My William James zone lasts much longer than Pace's. I get fired up, and it takes me a long time to calm down. At first, I felt bad about this because Pace gets over her anger quickly while I stay upset. We then learned about anger being physical, and realized that it's not a *problem*, it's a difference. My threshold is longer.

Now we have tools to help bring me out of the zone *before* I fall into the feedback loop and start random arguments to feed my fires. After we reach resolution, Pace will double-check with me. She'll ask how I'm feeling and if I need to go over things again. Often, rehashing why I was upset and what resolution was reached is an effective way to remind myself that everything is now okay. She'll hug me because physical touch reminds me how much I love her and how little I want to be angry at her. Touch has the added benefit of reminding my *body* that things are good, which helps break the loop. We'll do something fun together; laughing is an excellent way to calm down.

Sometimes, we fail to take these steps. We get distracted, we end happily but abruptly, or Pace makes the usual error and forgets that my William James zone is longer than hers. Sometimes in these situations, Pace will notice the anger I'm still holding in my body and ask what's up, providing me with a chance to connect with myself. Often I'll reply with, "I'm still in the zone. I need a little time."

Sometimes I can feel the zone taking hold even before we start to argue. I'll get physically angry; my heart will start pounding, my eyebrows go down, sometimes I cross my arms, sometimes I cry. I can feel the feedback loop start: my body gets upset, so my brain finds a reason for the upset, and I'll pick a fight with her if I'm not careful. When this happens, I can often catch myself, apologize, back off, and let her know that I was trapped in the zone. It's certainly not an excuse to be nasty, but it helps me understand what's happening.

For me, remembering that my zone is way longer than Pace's really helps. I'm not broken or wrong or sick, simply different. Knowing the length of our zones helps us to communicate better and to take more gentle care of each other.

Last but not least, remember to cut yourself and your partner some slack! Remember that we are made of meat. If you get angry, that's okay. In fact, it's healthy to express your anger rather than repress it. It's a natural part of the way people are made. Everyone feels anger, everyone experiences the William James zone, and different people (regardless of gender or other stereotypes) have different William James thresholds. Having a longer or shorter threshold doesn't make you a better or worse person. The important thing is to be aware of it. Knowing about the William James zone can improve your life.

Chapter 25:
The lollipop

The lollipop is a metaphor we use to explain the nature of expectations, attachment, and disappointment.[1] We'll illustrate it by comparing and contrasting three stories.

Claire's Example:
A Baseline

Claire has a lollipop. It's about two hundred licks of tasty lollipop. So she's standing around, licking on this lollipop, and eventually it's gone. She's eaten the whole lollipop, so now all she has left is a stick. She feels pretty happy; she enjoys lollipops, and she's finished a good one. She feels content.

The next story starts the same way, but ends differently.

---

1   We adapted the lollipop story from the book *Ancient Wisdom, New Spirit* by Peter Ralston.

Claire's Example: Dropped!

Claire has a lollipop, and she's licking it. Her lollipop is about half gone when she sneezes and accidentally drops it into a sewer drain! Now she feels disappointed, angry, frustrated, and indignant. After all, she had a good hundred more licks to go on that thing! She feels unsettled and unhappy.

There's one more story to go.

Claire's Example: Bonus!

Claire doesn't have a lollipop. She's minding her own business when her friend Anna comes up to her. Anna has a lollipop and says, "Hey, I have this great lollipop! I know you love lollipops, so would you like to share it? Here, have half and then I'll have the rest."

Claire accepts, enjoys half of the lollipop, and then she returns the second half to Anna. Here,

Claire feels better than content; she feels great! Bonus lollipop! What a good friend Anna is, to share her lollipop with Claire.

We have three stories here with three different outcomes, but what about these situations causes the results to vary so widely? In the "Bonus" story, Claire got *less* lollipop than she did in the "Baseline" story, yet she felt happier. In "Dropped", she had the same amount of lollipop as in "Bonus", yet she felt *miserable!* Let's look at that again:

Story	*Objective Outcome*	*Emotional Reaction*
"Baseline"	Claire ate the whole lollipop.	She felt content.
"Dropped"	Claire ate half of the lollipop.	She felt very upset.
"Bonus"	Claire ate half of the lollipop.	She felt very happy!

The objective outcomes of the last two stories are exactly the same (Claire ate half of a lollipop) and yet she had radically different emotional reactions! What causes the difference? The answer is expectation and attachment. In the "Baseline" story,

The lollipop

Claire expected to eat the whole lollipop, and her expectations were met. In "Dropped", she expected to eat the whole lollipop, but that didn't happen — she only got half. In the "Bonus" story, she also only got half of a lollipop, but since she had no expectations, anything was great!

We can now fill in the missing column of our table: expectations.

Story	Expectations	Objective Outcome	Reaction
"Baseline"	to eat a lollipop	She ate a whole lollipop.	Content.
"Dropped"	to eat a lollipop	She ate half a lollipop.	Very upset.
"Bonus"	none	She ate half a lollipop.	Very happy!

Now it becomes clear. Claire felt content when her expectations were met, she felt very upset when her expectations were violated, and she felt very happy when her expectations were exceeded.

Expectation is the assumption of the presence of something in the future. We begin to view what we expect as a thing we can have or get upset about not having. After all, it wasn't the loss of the *lollipop* that caused Claire's upset in "Dropped", it was the loss of the *expectation* of the lollipop. After all, Claire "lost" half of a lollipop in the "Bonus" story (by giving it back) and she ended up the happiest!

However, expectations don't explain everything. We could expect to do some onerous task, or something neutral and uninteresting, and the violation of that expectation wouldn't trouble us at all. For example, if we expected traffic to be bad tomorrow, we wouldn't be upset if we were wrong. In order to become upset over the loss of expectation, we must also be *attached* to the expectation; we must *want* our expectation to come true.

When we are attached to an expectation and that expectation is violated, something happens. In a fascinating kind of mental alchemy, expectation is transformed into upset.

Kyeli's Story: Motivation and Money

When we moved into our last apartment, we paid a hefty security deposit. We lived there only eight months and did minimal damage to our apartment. We expected the return of our entire security deposit when we moved out. We were relying on the extra money to help pay our moving expenses.

When we moved out, the landlord informed us we'd only be getting back half of our deposit! I was *furious!* I expected the entire deposit and he *stole* the other half from me! I held on to the loss of my (money) lollipop. In this case, the loss of it motivated me to do something about it. I called and wrote letters to the complex. I fought their decision. Eventually, the outcome changed in my favor; I got the other half of my deposit returned to me. Holding on to my attachment, to my expectation of getting my entire deposit back, helped me because it motivated me to fight for what I expected, and I got it!

That's not always the case, though. Recently, I miscalculated my spending money and wound up losing $50 I expected to have. I had plans for that money, and suddenly having $50 less than I expected upset me. I ranted and railed against the injustice of my bad math and I wound up in tears... but for all my ranting and raving, I couldn't recover the lost money. I eventually chose to let go of my attachment to the $50 lollipop so I could continue my life without being continuously upset by the loss of the money I'd expected to have.

In this case, holding on to my attachment to that $50 would have only caused me grief. I'd lost it, and there was no getting it back, no matter how motivated I was. I did get some good out of it: I created a monthly spreadsheet with formulas to keep track of my spending so this sort of mistake won't happen again.

In situations like these, our attachments and expectations get tangled up with motivation, desire, and the absence of what we've lost. We lose the lollipop, but we haven't lost the desire for the lollipop. This disrupts our internal harmony, and in response, we will cling tightly to whatever we have left. Usually, what we have left is the *absence* of the lollipop, the fact of losing it. This absence becomes at least as important to us as what we lost in the first place.

This can spur action: if Claire's lollipop were stolen instead of dropped, she might be motivated into taking the lollipop back (a useful action) but unfortunately, the feelings of loss and frustration can persist whether or not it is possible to correct the situation. When Claire dropped her lollipop into the sewer, there was nothing she could do about it, yet her upset feelings remained. In fact, the feelings tend to persist even if the situation is immediately corrected. If someone snatches your lollipop and you snatch it back right away, you won't feel fine and contented. Despite the fact that the outcome is now exactly as it was before, you're still likely to feel angry that someone tried to take your lollipop!

Despite all this anger, frustration, and attachment, you can choose another possible outcome. If you are aware that you are "holding onto a lollipop" and you find no reason to keep holding on, it is possible to let go of the absence of what you've lost.

When you feel resentment, bitterness, anger, or upset at the loss of something, you can ask yourself these questions:

"What is my lollipop in this situation?"

"Can I get it back, or am I holding onto this absence without purpose?"

"Is feeling upset serving me at all?"

"When I take away this absence that I'm focusing on, what does my situation look like?"

"What is the objective outcome?"

"Am I ready to let this go now?"

What you've lost doesn't have to be tangible; spending time with someone, for instance, is a common lollipop. It doesn't even have to be something you ever really had; you can feel upset about losing something you expected to have in the future.

Remember that the outcome of the "Dropped" story was the same as the outcome of the "Bonus" story: Claire ate half of a lollipop. In "Dropped," she felt upset, disappointed, and angry. In "Bonus," she felt happy. Since the objective outcomes are the same, there's nothing but her attitude that keeps her from choosing to be in the "Bonus" story instead of in the "Dropped" story. All she needs to do is let go.

Pace's Story: Missed Connection

I booked a flight to Origins, a gaming convention that I had enjoyed attending for the three years previous. On Friday, I got ready to leave, but then realized to my horror that my flight was booked for *Thursday*, not Friday! I called the airline but they said there was nothing they could do. I could get a partial refund but I couldn't get to Origins that weekend without spending a ridiculous amount of money.

I was incredibly disappointed! I felt angry at myself, angry at the airline, and bitterly envious of all my friends who were enjoying themselves at the convention. I had planned to split the cost of a room with one of my friends and I felt really bad for letting him down. The fun weekend I'd hoped for had turned into a fiasco of disappointment.

But then, after a couple of hours of feeling bad, I remembered the story of the lollipop. I imagined another story, a story in which I chose to take some time off work to spend with friends and family, and have a nice long weekend. I chose to be in that story instead. I let go of my absence-of-Origins lollipop, and you know what? I had a lovely weekend!

It's okay to choose to hang on to your absence-of-lollipop. Expectations and attachments are part of being human, and part of being connected to the world around us. However, isn't it nice to have the option to let go? By choosing a different story to be in, we create the possibility of happiness where before there was sadness, and we give ourselves a chance to better understand our own situations and motivations.

That's even better than a lollipop.

Chapter 26:

What do I get out of being right?

Our desire to be right can cloud our judgment. It can make us act harshly, unfairly, or angrily. It can even make us follow through with something we no longer want to do, simply so we can feel right. At times like this it helps to ask yourself, *"What do I get out of being right?"* The answer might surprise you and you might end up making a decision that will make you happier in the long run.

As with most things, it's a matter of perspective. We're taught that being wrong is bad and shameful. We learn to maintain an illusion of infallibility even when we're insecure on the inside. It's no wonder we get attached to being right — or more precisely, to being perceived as right.

Pace's Story: Privacy vs. Secrecy

There's a moment that sometimes happens to me in the middle of an argument. It's the moment when I suddenly realize that I'm wrong. I might keep arguing, I might even go on to "win," but deep down I know I've already lost — I knew it the moment that sinking feeling hit me in the pit of my stomach. Still, it can be tough to stop, to let it go. I feel like I *lost* and that makes me a *loser.* I'll tell you a story of a time when the moment hit me hard, and what happened when I kept fighting anyway.

Kyeli and I were discussing the difference between privacy and secrecy. I'd been having some email conversations with someone else, and when Kyeli asked what we were talking about, I got huffy and defensive, saying, "It's private."

She seemed confused and said, "But in our wedding vows, we promised not to have secrets from each other."

"It's not *secret,* Kyeli, it's *private.*"

"Well, if you don't want to share it with me, that seems like a secret from my point of view."

"If you trusted me, you would respect my privacy, and you wouldn't need me to tell you what I'm talking about with friends in email conversations!"

It only got worse from there. I tried to explain the difference between privacy and secrecy, but I wasn't doing a good job because I felt defensive. I didn't care about helping Kyeli understand as much as I cared about *being right.*

But then the moment struck. I had put all this effort into bolstering my defenses, building up my towers of reason and logic and definitions, but when the moment hit, it suddenly all felt hollow. And when my arguments rang hollow to myself, I was finally forced to look within — to look for the *true* reason that I was acting so hostile and defensive.

The true reason was that I felt that I was doing something wrong.

I thought that the email conversation had gone into (or maybe a little past) the gray area near the boundaries of what Kyeli and I had agreed was okay. We had an agreement in place to tell each other about important things, and the email conversation had gradually crossed the line over to important. I felt that I had trespassed on forbidden ground, so I was just trying to cover my ass so I wouldn't get caught.

All this talk about privacy and secrecy — this entire conversation — had been beating around the bush of what was actually going on. Yes, I value privacy, but in this case it was just a convenient defense to hide from the real issue.

But I couldn't admit that to myself. Even though the moment struck, even though I felt the sinking feeling in the pit of my stomach, I couldn't face the possibility of *being wrong*. So I turned back to my walls and towers and definitions and continued to fight.

Fifteen minutes and many hurt feelings later, I finally asked myself, *"What am I getting out of being right?"* The answer in this case was "Nothing worth all this hurt and conflict, and nothing worth avoiding the real issue." So I gave up the ghost.

Kyeli, who had been hurt by my verbal attacks, was understandably in the William James zone, so it took her a while to get into a place where she could listen. But after that, when I felt ready to talk about the real issue and she felt ready to listen, everything got better. I apologized for being defensive and hurting her. I admitted what I felt I had done wrong and we talked about it in detail. We talked about privacy and secrecy, and we understood each other! Now that I was no longer attached to being right, honest and open communication flowed freely.

Now that we were back on the same team, we were able to work things out in a way that met both our needs. I got to keep my privacy and we got rid of anything that smelled of secrecy. It ended up win/

win, all because I asked myself "What do I get out
of being right?"

What does being right really *mean?* What do we actually win?

There are two common answers to these questions, one based in self-esteem and one based in the esteem of others. When we are right, we feel good about ourselves. We feel validated. We feel that we are smart and that we have good judgment. Those are nice feelings. Also, when we are right, others think highly of us. We learn that others are more likely to respect us and think well of us if we're consistently correct.

When the answer to "What do I get out of being right?" is "I get to feel good about myself," the problem boils down to a balancing of desires. Insisting that you are right may hurt your partner's feelings. Insisting that you are right may blind you to something useful that your partner is saying. On one hand, how great are these risks? On the other hand, how important is feeling good about yourself? Consider the relative importance of these things, and you will know what to do.

When the answer to "What do I get out of being right?" is "I get the respect of others," the problem again boils down to a balancing of desires. Is the respect of others the most important thing to you in this situation? Or does what *you* want outweigh what others might think?

Allison & Billy and

Corey & Donovan's Example:

Religion vs. Polka

Allison and Billy have stress in their relationship because they practice different religions and can't agree about how to raise their future children. Their friends Corey and Donovan have stress in their relationship because Corey adores polka dancing and wants to dance it with Donovan, but Donovan can't stand polka.

Allison breaks up with Billy. She feels justified because she knows her friends will support her decision. People generally recognize religious differences as a "big deal" and as a justifiable reason to break up with someone. Allison will be perceived as *being right*, so she's not afraid to break up with Billy.

Corey chooses not to break up with Donovan. She fears that her friends would not support her if she did dump him. People don't generally consider polka a "big deal," so Corey fears being ridiculed by her friends, *even though polka is more important to Corey than religion is to Allison.* Corey would *not* be perceived as being right, and her fear of that was strong enough to keep her in an unhappy relationship.

Asking yourself, "What do I get out of being right?" doesn't work if you presume the answer. Sometimes the answer will be "nothing, really" and you can choose to let go of your attachment to being right with little effort. However, sometimes what you get out of being right is important: a more stable relationship, acknowledgment of a job well done, or deeper trust.

Kyeli's Story: Being Right About Nalia

I'm usually not attached to being right; I'm more interested in resolving conflict and moving toward everyone feeling better. For a long time, I couldn't understand what was so important about being right, nor could I understand others' attachment to it.

Then, a situation occurred which made me get it. Pace was interested in dating this girl, Nalia. Neither of us knew Nalia well, but what I knew of her was negative. I felt like she was nothing but bad news and that adding her to our lives would only cause trouble.

Pace and I argued over this for several weeks. We went on and on, back and forth. I wanted to be right! And when I asked myself what I was going to get out of being right, the answer was "a healthier, happier, more stable relationship with Pace." I remained firm in my stance on Nalia.

After a while, Nalia made it easier for me. In an email to Pace, she expressly stated several blatantly false things about me, and told Pace that, if she was smart, she'd end her relationship with me and get out while she still could. Pace read the email, discussed it with me, and realized that I had been right all along. Nalia did not respect our relationship and was clearly out to make things between me and Pace rocky, if not end things altogether. Pace chose to end her friendship with Nalia and we went on with our lives.

What if you ask yourself, "What am I getting out of being right?" and the answer is simply "not being wrong"? Relax! There's nothing wrong with being wrong. Everyone is wrong sometimes; it's not possible to be right 100% of the time. Being the one who "knows what's right" for someone else is often a way to force your opinions and way of thinking on them.

Regardless of the answer you find when you ask yourself what you get out of being right, the most important thing is for your answer to be *true*. Simply asking the question can help give you a better understanding of your motivations, and that will help you make better decisions.

CHAPTER 27:

REFLECTION

"Oh, wow, is that what you heard?"

Communication is a tricky process, fraught with the peril of misunderstanding. Successful communication requires four separate steps. To illustrate, imagine that you and your friend Daniel are having a conversation; Daniel talks and you listen.

Step 1. Daniel has a concept that he wants to express. He translates this into words.

Step 2. He speaks the words.

Step 3. You hear the words.

Step 4. Based on your interpretation of the words you heard, you make your best guess at the concept Daniel had in Step 1.

Any one of these four steps can go wrong. Step 1 could go wrong if Daniel fails to capture his intent accurately with the words he chooses. Step 2 could go wrong if he accidentally stumbles over his words. Step 3 could go wrong if you mishear the words he spoke. Step 4 could go wrong if you incorrectly guess Daniel's intent or meaning.

With all these possibilities for error, it's a wonder successful communication ever happens at all! One way to make communication more successful is to add a Step 5: *Reflection*.

Step 5. You rephrase what you heard in your own words. If Daniel thinks that wasn't actually what he intended, the two of you go around again and clarify.

Reflection is saying "Here's what I heard you say." People don't often take time for this extra step, because most people don't realize how often miscommunication happens. If you reflect what you just heard back to the person who said it, many occurrences of the usual error and other communication mistakes can be caught before they escalate into misunderstanding or conflict. It can also work the other way, too. When you notice miscommunication has occurred, you can use reflection to get to the bottom of the misunderstanding.

Kyeli's Story: Why Am I Doing This?

For a long time, I didn't understand reflection. I thought it was unimportant and kind of annoying. But then I realized that we each speak our own version of our native language. If I say, "Please get some grapes at the store" to Pace, she probably hears me well enough. However, her idea of "some" might be vastly different than mine; maybe she thinks "a pound" and I mean "five pounds" (though that would be a lot of grapes). And this is just one of hundreds of ways we can miscommunicate! Reflection can't solve all miscommunications, but it can cut a lot of them short.

What drove this home for me was when my coworker Melony and I were working together to get a newsletter out and she wanted me to finish it for her. She gave me a list of instructions. I repeated back to her what I'd heard her ask me to do. "You want me to write out your schedule for the next two months, talk about the special event on Monday the 24th, include that example from Bob's funeral, and end with the anecdote from Mary's sister." She listened, gave me a long, weird look, then said, "I know that's what I *said*, but that's not really what I want." She gave me a different set of directions: "I want you to create a table with my calendar for the next month, highlight Monday the 24th and mention the special event, omit the example from Bob's funeral, and end with the anecdote from Gloria's sister; I don't like the one Mary's sister sent now that I'm re-reading it." "Okay," I began, "let's go over that again. You want the calendar for the next month in a table, a simple highlight and mention of the Monday event, no funeral example, and the story from Gloria's sister." This time, she approved them and I went on to do the work. This interaction saved me a lot of work and hassle, and saved Melony a lot of frustration at having my time spent doing the wrong thing!

Reflection ensures that your communication is received with your intent intact. Imagine you are communicating using a mirror. A smooth mirror reflects correctly, but a warped one can cause misunderstanding. It is useful to have a tool to know whether you've been understood or not, right away, before miscommunication has a chance to cause any problems.[1]

---

1   You can find more information on reflection, also known as "active listening" or "paraphrasing," in many other books on communication, including *Nonviolent Communication: A Language of Life* by Marshall Rosenberg.

CHAPTER 28:
VERBAL AIKIDO

Do you ever feel attacked by someone? Not punched or kicked, but attacked with words, expressions, or emotions? We certainly have. In this chapter, we'll explain how you can take the principles of aikido, which deal with physical attacks, and apply those same principles to verbal attacks as well, using *verbal aikido*.[1]

There are six basic ways to respond to a verbal attack. They correspond to the six ways of responding to a physical attack. Each one can be a useful response depending on the situation. The six responses are:

1. Fighting Back

Someone attacks you and you attack them in return. It's simple.

---

1   We learned about verbal aikido by reading *Aikido in Everyday Life: Giving in to Get Your Way* by Terry Dobson and Victor Miller. We highly recommend it!

Attacker: You lazy so-and-so, you didn't do the dishes and now we've got no clean plates. You never do anything right!

You: Shut up and get off my back!

You can use Fighting Back as a last resort, but it usually ends with everyone involved getting hurt. It is as likely to create conflict as it is to end it. We often choose Fighting Back when we don't realize that we have a choice. When you experience an impulse to fight back, consider the other five responses before acting.

2. Withdrawal

Someone attacks you and you retreat.

Attacker: You lazy so-and-so, you didn't do the dishes and now we've got no clean plates. You never do anything right!

You: Look, I don't have time to talk about this right now; I'm in the middle of studying for my finals. (goes off to finish studying)

Withdrawal, though much-maligned, is a useful strategy for when the time and place are simply wrong, or for when nothing else works and you have an escape route open.

3. Parley

Someone attacks you and you look for a compromise.

> *Attacker:* You lazy so-and-so, you didn't do the dishes and now we've got no clean plates. You never do anything right!

> *You:* I've been swamped recently. Maybe we can work out a rotation to help us both?

The strength of Parley lies in give-and-take, trying to find a fair resolution for both parties. It's often the best option possible when you and your attacker are ultimately not on the same team.

4. Doing Nothing

Someone attacks you and you do nothing.

> *Attacker:* You lazy so-and-so, you didn't do the dishes and now we've got no clean plates. You never do anything right!

> *You:* (says nothing and waits)

In some situations, especially when the attack makes no sense, Doing Nothing is the most useful response possible. It gives you time to formulate a response and can help you find out what's actually behind an attack. Your attacker may feel compelled to fill the silence, giving you more information about what they are thinking or why they attacked you.

5. Deception

Someone attacks you and you deceive or distract them.

> *Attacker:* You lazy so-and-so, you didn't do the dishes and now we've got no clean plates. You never do anything right!

> *You:* My... carpal tunnel is acting up today.

Deception is a limited response. It never solves a problem; it only buys a little time. Use Deception when you think that distracting your attacker might defuse their attack or to avoid an ill-timed conversation. We don't care for Deception much because we value openness and honesty, but it can be useful in some situations. A woman once told her attempted rapist that she had a venereal disease and he left her alone. That was certainly a good use of deception.

6. Aiki

Someone attacks you and you turn to see things from their point of view.

> *Attacker:* You lazy so-and-so, you didn't do the dishes and now we've got no clean plates. You never do anything right!

> *You:* Yeah, it really sucks to come home to a sink full of dirty dishes, especially when you asked me to do them. I can see why you're upset!

This is the big one. Aiki is by far the most useful and effective response to an attack; it creates a win/win situation.

People usually attack because they feel upset. They feel unhappy and attack you to somehow make it better. *Every attack is a cry for help.* With Aiki, you can give them that help, protect yourself from attack, and improve your interpersonal relationships, all at the same time!

Here's what happens when you use Aiki: Someone attacks you, but you are not there being attacked; you are seeing things from their point of view, hearing their words, and showing them that you understand their feelings. It is important to note that you *do not have to agree* in order to use Aiki; all you need to do is to acknowledge that your attacker's feelings are valid.

At that point, there's generally a pause as the person notices that their attack isn't hitting anything, that the fight they expected isn't materializing. People don't know how to react to that, so their surprise manifests as a distinct pause. After that pause, you can gently lead them toward the real issue and work together to solve the problem. Aiki transforms conflict into harmony.

Aiki requires not only empathy, but also some practice putting that empathy into words. Here's an example of an exchange that is *not* Aiki:

> *Attacker:* You lazy so-and-so, you didn't do the dishes and now we've got no clean plates. You never do anything right!

> *You:* Yeah, I can see why you'd be mad. You're right, I *am* lazy and I never do anything right. I'm a worthless hunk of slime, just like this hunk of slime right here on this dirty dish.

That's not Aiki, that's self-deprecation. It's a veiled form of Fighting Back; you're implying, "My attacker is a bad, mean person for beating up on helpless little me." Your attacker doesn't feel understood or heard, but instead feels frustrated or angry. They might even feel like they have to defend you from yourself.

If you're not careful, sometimes Aiki can come across as condescending or holier-than-thou:

> *Attacker:* You lazy so-and-so, you didn't do the dishes and now we've got no clean plates. You never do anything right!

> *You:* I can see how you would feel that way. You expected me to do the dishes and you got attached to that expectation. No wonder you're feeling angry; I don't blame you for that. After all, expectations and attachments are part of being human.

> *Attacker:* Oh, aren't you such a mighty guru, taking pity on poor lowly me for having feelings! (throws dish)

It's important to come across with empathy rather than pity. If you sound condescending, your attacker will react with more anger and you won't get anywhere. This works best, naturally, if you're feeling empathy rather than pity. Remember, you don't have to agree with your attacker, but you do have to put yourself in their shoes and make a clear attempt to understand.

Even with the best knowledge combined with the best intent, sometimes you still won't be able to get through if the other person isn't willing to listen to you, but we've found Aiki to have the best chance of success in most circumstances.

Nonverbal communication is also important in Aiki:

> *Attacker:* (points accusingly) You lazy so-and-so, you didn't do the dishes and now we've got no clean plates. You never do anything right!

> *You:* (arms at sides, palms open) Yeah, it really sucks to come home to a sink full of dirty dishes. (takes a soft step toward Attacker and looks into Attacker's eyes) I can see why you'd be mad. (gently takes Attacker's hand)

Just as different people have different verbal communication styles, different people have different nonverbal communication styles. For example, some people may not want to be touched when they're angry. If you know your attacker well, you can communicate both verbally and nonverbally in the way you think will be most effective for that person.

Kyeli's Story: Not Enough Blue!

I ordered a sculpture from an online store. I'd wanted it for a decade and I finally had the means to procure it. I felt *extremely* happy and eagerly awaited its arrival. When it did arrive, I opened it up, only to discover that the coloration was quite different than I had expected.

I felt dismayed. I went to the store's website in a huff, looking for an email address so I could send a lengthy complaint. Instead, I found a phone number and decided that making my complaint via phone would be even more satisfying. I made the call.

I started off by saying that I had a problem with my recent order. The shopkeeper said, "Well, tell me all about it and we'll see how we can fix it."

I was all ready to launch into a lengthy tirade. I began with, "I bought this sculpture. Upon its arrival I discovered that the coloration is wrong."

The man on the phone made sympathetic noises and said, "I know what it feels like to expect one thing and get something different. How disappointing! Let's look at other examples of the sculpture together and see if we can find one that better matches your expectations."

Boom! Immediately, I went from angry and ready for a fight to calm and ready to work things out in a helpful manner. I spent several minutes on the phone, we came to a pleasant conclusion, and I disconnected in a good mood.

It wasn't until I was describing the situation later to Pace that she pointed out the shopkeeper had used Aiki with me. He had listened to my complaint, sympathized with my feelings, and worked with me to make things better. I felt heard and understood right from the start, and this enabled us to communicate effectively and pleasantly.

Aiki will not work unless it comes from the heart. If you try to use Aiki manipulatively to avoid a conflict, that's Deception and not Aiki. Your attacker may perceive that they are not being truly heard or understood and will continue to fight.

Kyeli's Story: It's Super Effective!

Aiki can calm me down in the midst of a real anger-ball moment. If I'm upset at Pace and she moves gently toward me, hands outstretched, voice low, compassion in her eyes, I know I'm being heard. She's listening to me and making every attempt to understand me. Even if she fails to understand me, she's *trying*. We're not against each other anymore even if I'm still hurt or angry. Often this will transform my anger into its real source — fear — and I'll start crying. Now, we can really begin to communicate and get to the bottom of what was hurting me from the start.

It works on me even though I can recognize when Pace is using it; it's that effective!

When Aiki is used from the heart, openly and honestly, it can stop a verbal attack right in its tracks. Think of a time when you've lashed out. What were you really feeling? Anger? Fear? Helplessness? When we're upset or angry, the first thing we need is to be heard. We need to express ourselves, to get our feelings out, and to know they were received. Aiki accomplishes this effectively and compassionately.

While we find all six of these techniques beneficial in some cases, for most situations we recommend Aiki — given honestly and from the heart — as the best response to a verbal attack.

PART V: POSITIVITY!

CHAPTER 29:

"THAT MAKES ME REALLY HAPPY!"

Have you ever noticed how much we focus on the negative? Think about it: when someone asks you how your day went, it may be hard to remember all the good things that happened to you. They fade into the background. On the other hand, any rough or stressful thing that happened that day will linger at the forefront of your mind, coloring your perception of the day.

Readers of blogs or online journals will know what we're talking about when we say that people are far more likely to write about the bad things in their life than the good. People often describe their journals as unintentionally displaying a one-sided, negative view of themselves.

Negative things vibrantly stand out in our minds and memories. There is a sound evolutionary reason for this: the person who clearly remembers their experience with the poisonous berries or the unpleasant events that occurred when wandering too close to a tiger's lair is more likely to avoid them in the future, thus increasing their chances of survival. As such, we have evolved with a part of the brain that is sensitive to negative emotions, called the amygdala.

The amygdala calculates the emotional significance of events, determines their impact in your memory, and amplifies your perceptions of emotionally significant events. Negative emotions get your amygdala going more than anything else.

Here we are, walking around in the world. There are no free-roaming tigers nearby and no poisonous berries in the grocery store. We're going about our lives and trying to be happy, but we've got the dice loaded against us! We're biologically primed to notice and remember the negative, so that becomes what we communicate. That becomes what we reinforce in ourselves and what we spread around to others.

The question then becomes "How do we counteract this effect?" One effective way we've found is to *habitually and frequently communicate the positive.*

Kyeli's Story: Happiness Squared

When Pace and I started dating, we had many email and telephone conversations, since we lived in different parts of the state. Often, she would exclaim, *"That makes me really happy!"* Gradually, I noticed that every time she said this, I felt happy, too! Also, I realized that it helped me focus on the things that made me happy in my day-to-day life. At first, I focused on happy events so that I could have joy to share with her (what a good reason in and of itself, sharing joy with a loved one), so it happened by accident. After a while, I came to realize that the simple act of saying "That makes me happy!" when something made me happy helped me remember the good parts of every day, rather than just the mundane or bad parts. When this realization struck me, I decided to intentionally state to myself and others, "That makes me happy!" whenever something did.

This one thing dramatically changed my life. I began to focus on the good rather than the bad. It brings kindness into my attitude and smiles to my face. Also, it's contagious: hearing me say, "That makes me really happy!" has brought awareness to my friends, and some of them say it now, too!

Try it! Whenever something makes you happy, say, "That makes me happy!" Whenever something makes you *really* happy, say, "That makes me really happy!" Say it out loud, even if no one is around to hear you. This is an easy way to reinforce your happiness and to share it with those around you. The simple act of speaking your happiness aloud will make it stand out in your memory and your experience. If you do this all the time, people who spend time with you may start picking it up too, spreading the happiness around. Joy shared is joy multiplied! Life is 10% of what happens to you and 90% of how you react to it.[1]

This simple phrase has significantly increased the amount of happiness in our lives. We highly recommend trying it out for just one month and experiencing the happiness it will bring to your life too. If it works for you too, that will make us really happy!

---

1 John Maxwell likes to say this, for instance in his book *Attitude 101*.

CHAPTER 30:

IT'S OKAY TO HAVE PROBLEMS

Here's another incredibly harmful lie we tell ourselves: we must be perfect to be desirable. If we're flawed, we feel like no one will want us around. This fear makes us do what we can to hide our flaws, our pain, our troubles, our *problems*, and try to show the world a perfect face. This lie is powerful and insidious.

We have bought into this lie so deeply that we will often hurt ourselves internally rather than deal with the situation that's bothering us.

Pace's Story:

Pace Needs More Alone Time

One random autumn day, I noticed that I felt a little antisocial and jittery. After some introspection, I realized that this was bubbling up because of a deeper issue: I wasn't getting enough time to myself.

"Damn! I have a *problem*," I thought to myself. I worried about the discomfort and potential conflict it would cause to bring it up. I worried about the stress of rearranging various logistics in our lives to fix my problem. Was it worth all the trouble?

I considered the alternative. "I can just pretend this isn't bothering me. I can get over it by myself without troubling anyone else. I'll be okay. I don't want to bother anyone. After all, it's me who woke up today with a *problem*, so I might as well take the responsibility for it."

I sighed, tried to ignore the problem, and returned to my regularly scheduled life.

This attitude is very harmful. We've learned this the hard way. We bought into the myth that it's not okay to be flawed, but the truth is that *it's okay to have problems.* If you ignore your problems, it not only harms you, it harms everyone who cares about you. You have friends or family who love you and want to help you, but by keeping your problems to yourself, you're denying them the opportunity. When you're on the same team and everyone shares the same goal, it doesn't matter who happens to have the problem this time. We each take turns having problems, and it's okay! The fact that you *have* a problem doesn't mean that you *are* a problem. If we think of problems as a fact of life, a fact of being a person, and a fact of all interpersonal relationships, we can escape from this harmful attitude.

Sometimes we don't feel safe talking about our problems. Sometimes, you know full well that bringing up what's bothering you will require a long, difficult conversation, and you don't feel up to it yet. You may be tempted to squelch, to delay, or to ignore, but remember that the only way out is through. The best way of dealing with this reluctance is to remember that it's okay for you to have problems and it's okay for your partner to have problems too.

It's okay to have problems communicating, too. When people miscommunicate, they rarely react by saying, "Oh well, miscommunication happens, let's move on and try again." Instead, they feel that they have been wronged, they react defensively, and conflict ensues. If you remember that it's okay to have problems, that it's okay to miscommunicate, then you *can* move on and try again.

It's okay to have problems! It doesn't make you a burden, it doesn't make you bad or wrong or stupid or annoying. Having problems is part of being human. We have triggers that spark emotional responses and set us off. We get hurt. We get scared. We get angry, upset, worried, and nervous. We cry. We yell. We make up, we talk, and we work through things. It's beautiful!

Pace's Story:

Pace Needs More Alone Time (Reprise)

One random winter day, I noticed that I felt a bit jittery and antisocial. After some introspection, I realized that these feelings were coming to the surface because of an underlying issue: I wasn't getting enough time to myself.

I thought to myself, "Crap, I have a *problem!* I had hoped this would go away, but here it is again. Oh no! This sucks." I stressed out about the conflict that might arise if I brought it up with Kyeli. I worried about logistics. I berated myself for failing to successfully get over the problem last time it came up.

But then I remembered a conversation that we had a couple of weeks ago. We said that *it's okay to have problems.* "Yeah. It's okay!" I shouted excitedly inside my head. "It doesn't mean that I'm bad or wrong; it doesn't mean that I *am* a problem. So let's work it out instead of ignoring it!"

I talked to Kyeli about the problem. There were stressful moments during the discussion, but she reminded me that we were on the same team, working to solve the problem together. In the end, we figured out a good schedule that met both of our needs and a good system for remembering the schedule.

Now the problem is solved and we're both getting what we need. I'm glad I remembered that it's okay to have problems!

CHAPTER 31:

KNOWING IS HALF THE BATTLE

Y ou can't solve a problem unless you first know it exists.
Often when we discover a problem, we react with dismay.
We say, "Oh no, now there's this new problem!" and feel
worse than we did before we discovered it. That's not the whole
story, though — you can't solve a problem unless you identify it
first. *Knowing is half the battle.*

Take a look at the illustration. This is what we call the Hill of Discovery. On the far left are the Flatlands of Stagnation. The steep drop at the end of the Flatlands is The Cliff, which leads down into The Pit. After that is the rough climb up the Hill of Discovery, leading up to the Plateau of Happiness.

We've seen this pattern over and over again in communication, problem solving, and self-improvement. In the illustration, horizontal distance indicates the passing of time and vertical distance indicates your level of happiness, higher being happier. You start out on the Flatlands of Stagnation. A lot of people get stuck there, either because they don't know there's anywhere to go from there or because they're afraid of The Cliff. Then, you either jump off The Cliff or are pushed off, and everything is suddenly horrible. Back in the Flatlands of Stagnation, everything was fine. You were complacent, you were happy with ignoring little problems, you were basically content. Now that you've fallen into The Pit, there are all these problems that you can't ignore anymore, you don't know what to do about them, and everything seems desperate and bleak.

Then, having nowhere to go but up, you face those problems. You think about them, you communicate about them, and you figure out what's at the root of them. You gain knowledge and insight about yourself, and about whoever or whatever else is involved. You've begun the long climb up the Hill of Discovery. It takes a lot of time and a lot of work, but eventually you pull yourself up out of The Pit, and soon you're higher up (happier) than you were when you were back in the Flatlands of Stagnation. You're solving your problems instead of ignoring them and making yourself happier along the way. Eventually you reach the top, the Plateau of Happiness, when your problems from The Pit have been resolved.

Our natural and understandable reaction when we fall into The Pit is to say, "Oh no! Everything is horrible!" We're judging our situation by the vertical distance: we were about halfway up and now we're at rock bottom. Surely we're worse off than we were before?

Here's another way of looking at it: you could judge your situation by the *horizontal* distance. Instead of being dismayed at having fallen into The Pit, say to yourself, "Now I'm one step closer to the Plateau of Happiness." It's true. The only way to the Plateau of Happiness is by jumping off The Cliff. We can never resolve our problems unless we first face them and admit they are problems; knowing is half the battle. When you're in The Pit, it's hard to see the silver lining, but we've found that keeping this picture in mind helps us remain positive and focused on the happiness to be gained in the future rather than the troubles we're experiencing in the present.

Kyeli's Story: The Oubliette

Sometimes I wind up stuck in The Pit, mired in my own problems. The light of understanding flickers, fades, and finally extinguishes, leaving me in darkness, surrounded by my own echoes. I struggle with a problem for so long I get trapped and lost; the pit becomes an oubliette and I've forgotten where I am.

I spend days, weeks, even months pacing back and forth, starving for resolution. I get bogged down with stress, fear, and unhappiness. Eventually, light returns like a bolt of lightning and I remember: I'm in The Pit! I say out loud, "It's okay! It's only The Pit!"

Suddenly, by saying that, by remembering where I am, The Pit doesn't seem so bad. No one ever stays there forever; being in The Pit means that once I get out, things will be much better. I hear the echoes lessen and I take those first precious steps up the Hill of Discovery back out into the sun.

Knowing you have a problem puts you further along the path of getting better, of feeling happier. Knowing you can fix it helps your mood and your attitude, and strengthens your ability to do something about it. Finding out something new about yourself, even when it's negative, is really a positive thing. Self-knowledge is wonderful! The only way out of the pit is to first know you're there; you can't heal without acknowledging the wound. Knowledge is power.

Chapter 32:

Rephrasing things positively

The words we use to describe our lives affect how we perceive our lives and thus the quality of our lives. You can improve the quality of your life by choosing to *rephrase things positively*. In particular, we've found that rephrasing obligation words, limitation words, and violent words has significantly improved our happiness, and we're going to show you why and how.

Obligation words

Sometimes we enter into obligations willingly, which is fine, but often people create tons of completely unnecessary obligation, thereby burdening themselves with heavy loads of stress.

There are lots of obligation-inducing words in English. Here are some examples:

should

ought

must

have to

need to

supposed to

forced to

Every time you use one of these words or phrases, you unintentionally take a little more obligation onto yourself. Why? There's so much obligation out there anyway, why choose to speak in such a way as to heap *more* of it onto yourself? It's harmful, it's completely unnecessary, and it's not even *honest*. The truth is that any obligation you have is self-imposed, because if you want something badly enough, you will do it. Conversely, if you don't want to do something, you'll find ways to avoid it. A feeling of "should" indicates a conflict between your wants: you want the end result, but you don't want to go through the process of getting it. You can rephrase this — and thereby reimagine it — by talking about it purely in terms of what you *want* to do instead of what you feel you *should* do.

Take, for example, "I should go to the store." What we actually mean is something like, "We are low on food, and I want to eat, so I'll go to the store so I can get what I want to eat." By using "should," we're putting obligation into it, making it into something we *don't* want to do. By removing "should," we turn it into something that is good for us and therefore less of an obligation and more of a good, happy-making thing. Here are some more examples:

Obligation-Inducing Phrasing	*Positive Rephrasing*
"I need to call my friend tonight."	"I want to call my friend tonight."
"I should get to bed by 11 tonight so I'm not sleepy and miserable all day tomorrow."	"I'd like to get to bed by 11 tonight so I'll be happy and awake tomorrow."
"I want to sleep in, but I can't because I have to go to work today."	"I want to sleep in, but I also want to keep my job, so I'll choose to go to work today because I want that more than I want to sleep in."

Feel how empowering these rephrasings are. Instead of presenting yourself as a hapless victim of fate, you're presenting yourself as the captain of your own destiny. *You* are the one making the choices, *you* are the one choosing to do what you want to do, *you* are the one choosing to do what makes you most happy.

"Should" pops up all over the place, so it's a good starting point to practice rephrasing things positively. It's easier to start with one word than to try to tackle the whole mess at once. We recommend being gentle with yourself, rephrasing each time you say "should"; for us this was a slow but successful process. You'll find yourself using "should" and other obligation words less and less, and even better, you'll find yourself *thinking* it less and less. Eventually, the word will sound odd when others say it!

Sometimes we found ourselves syntactically replacing "should" with "it would be good to," so we chose to eliminate that phrase as well. Who says it would be good? Me? If so, then I'll say, "It would make me happy to" or "I want to" instead. Often it's covering up for "(Society says) it would be good to," and that's another form of obligation.

After practicing for a few months, especially if you have a positive-rephrasing buddy doing it alongside you so you can catch each other, you can completely eliminate all of these words and phrases from your vocabulary. We try to set a good example; the only place you'll see the word "should" in this entire book is in this chapter where we're talking about it explicitly. We've done this successfully, we're profoundly happier for it, and you can do it too. Some rephrasings are challenging, but most of them are *so easy* that you'll wonder why anyone would choose to say things in a negative or obligation-inducing way. It's insidious.

Limitation Words

There's another insidious set of words that we use to chain ourselves down with unnecessary limitations. Here are some examples:

> can't
>
> impossible
>
> too hard
>
> never
>
> not good enough

Most of the time you use these words, they don't apply at all. In truth, you *can* do anything you put your mind to. This isn't an empty platitude, this is scientific fact. How does it serve you to be anything less than your full potential? How does it make you happier or more fulfilled to trick yourself into thinking you're less capable than you actually are? One good way to unlock yourself from these chains is to stop using the words that reinforce your perceived limitations.

Take, for example, "I could never play the piano that well; I'm just not good enough." It's time to expose yet another myth propagated by our culture: *the myth of talent.* Science has proven this to be a myth; the number one factor in how good you are at something is neither talent nor upbringing, it is simply the amount of *effortful practice* you put into it.[1] "Practice makes perfect" is not just a cliché, it has been scientifically proven, so why not say, "I could play the piano well if I wanted to devote three or four years to practicing, but I'm choosing to spend my time on other things instead." Not only is that phrasing more positive and more likely to make you happier and feel better about yourself, it's *more true.*

Kyeli's Story: The Piano Myth

When I was young, I wanted to learn to play the piano. I love the music it makes and I wanted to be able to accompany myself when I sing. When I expressed my desire to learn to an instructor, she said I would *never* be able to play piano. I have short fingers, utterly unsuitable. I was so discouraged! I took in her words and wove them as part of my life story. I began saying "I *can't* play piano."

When we started rephrasing things, I mentioned this to Pace. Suddenly, I was filled with the knowledge that I *can* play the piano, if I really want to

---

1   A lot of study has been done on expertise and effortful practice. If you're interested in learning more, check out the *Cambridge Handbook of Expertise and Expert Performance*, by Ericsson, Charness, Feltovich, and Hoffman, in particular chapter 2.1.

do so! I can overcome any limitations with enough practice. I *can* play the piano!

Then I thought it over further. Is playing the piano something I really want to spend time learning? I decided no, it's not... but that's *my choice!* So now I say, "I can play the piano if I want to learn, but I choose not to spend my time learning that."

I want to impress upon you, dear reader, the power that has given me. Changing that one phrase in my life, changing that "can't" to a "can," has made me feel stronger and more capable than almost anything else I've ever done. I learned how to be a good speller — I stopped saying, "I can't spell," and almost overnight realized that I can, in fact, spell quite well. I stopped saying, "I can't do math" and found that, while not a whiz at it, I can do quite a lot of math. I stopped saying, "I can't write well" and have written this book, not to mention the many stories I've since written!

I feel better about myself as well as feeling more capable. I know I *can* do anything. Knowing and saying that the things I "can't" do are things I'm really choosing not to do empowers me and helps me own my life, rather than feel like a helpless victim.

Here are some more examples of rephrasing limiting words more positively.

Limiting Phrasing	*Positive Rephrasing*
"I'm a horrible cook."	"I haven't chosen to spend much time cooking, so I'm not very well-practiced at it."

Rephrasing things positively

Limiting Phrasing	Positive Rephrasing
"I suck at math."	"I'm not great at math because I haven't spent much time studying it, and I don't want to because I don't enjoy it at all."
"It's impossible for me to be honest *all* the time; I'm a Scorpio!"	"I sometimes choose to be dishonest, but that's my responsibility and I could choose otherwise if I wished to."
"I can't go to the movies, I don't have enough time! I have to work!"	"I'm choosing to prioritize my work over going to a movie right now."
"I can't make it to your party, because I... uh... have plans."	"I appreciate the invitation, but I'm more in the mood to stay home and relax instead."

Notice how each limiting phrase has been rephrased in terms of *wants* and *choices*. Here's an example that ties in with "I" statements:

Limiting Phrasing	Positive Rephrasing
"You made me mad by doing that."	"I felt mad when you did that."

The truth revealed by this rephrasing is that we choose our reactions to events, even our emotional reactions. This can be frightening but also empowering.

Like obligation words, limiting words trick you into giving up your own power. When you use these words, you give up responsibility for your actions. Rephrasing things positively helps you be more empowered and more honest.

Pace's Story: "I'm Not Very Observant"

I used to always say, "I'm just not very observant" whenever I would fail to notice something. "Being oblivious is part of my nature," I'd repeat whenever the subject came up. Even when my failure to observe something ended up causing lots of problems, I would stick to my guns and insist that it was a basic, unchangeable part of my nature.

One day, a few months after we had started rephrasing things positively, I decided that being unobservant was no longer serving me and I chose to change. Kyeli drove me home from work. As I got out of the car, I said, "I have a surprise for you, Kyeli. I'm observant now. Please catch me if you notice me saying that I'm unobservant or oblivious." And from that moment on, I've been observant. It didn't take practice or time, all it took was a firm desire to change and a commitment to stay that way. You can do this too! Pay attention to the false limits you set for yourself. See if you want to change any of them. And if you do, you can choose to change in an instant! All you need to do is make up your mind.

Violent Words

We've also chosen to rephrase violent words. In the past, we used phrases like:

I'll kick your ass if you...

Don't make me hurt you...

It makes me want to smack you when you...

I'm gonna beat the crap out of you if you...

When we used these words, it was almost always teasingly, but for the same reasons we don't like teasing, we also didn't like this pattern in our communication. The two reasons we chose to rephrase these words are that we like to avoid violence and we also like to avoid dishonesty. Words that imply violence when none is truly intended are dishonest; we now use phrases like "I feel angry when..." or "I would feel unhappy if..." which are less violent and more true. It feels good to weed these words out of our vocabularies; such harmful language is unpleasant both to hear and to say. Rephrasing these words had an unexpected bonus; we became less physically violent as our words became less violent. Playful yet painful smacks slowly stopped and we became more aware of how we treat each other. We started treating each other the way we wanted to, instead of the way we were used to — and that's a powerful difference.

The power of words to shape thought isn't limited to obligation words, limitation words, and violent words. Once you start practicing rephrasing things positively, you may find other categories of words that you want to rephrase as well. We mention these three categories explicitly because all these rephrasings have significantly improved the quality of our lives, and they can improve yours too! We suggest you start with rephrasing "should," with a buddy if possible, and see how that works for you. It takes some practice, but we've found it to be well worth the effort.

CHAPTER 33:

TEASING

Teasing is a common element in communication, even among adults. Let's take a closer look at teasing and find out what is actually going on.

Stephanie's Example: Don't Tease My Hair!

Stephanie gets a perm. It looks odd and frizzy. She asks her friend Alice's opinion, and Alice says, "It looks like you stuck your finger in an electrical outlet!" She laughs, then says, "Just kidding." But despite that, Stephanie's feelings are hurt. Alice gets annoyed; after all, she was only teasing. "What's wrong with you, Stephanie?" Alice retorts. "Can't you take a joke?" Alice turns to her other friends for support and they band together to defend Alice. "You're so sensitive, Stephanie! Alice was just teasing; she didn't mean anything by it!"

What actually happened in this story? Let's break it down and take a closer look.

Stephanie gets a perm. It looks odd and frizzy. She asks her friend Alice's opinion, and Alice says, "It looks like you stuck your finger in an electrical outlet!"

If the story ended here, what would you think of Alice? Would you think she was being a good friend to Stephanie? Would you think she was being mean and hurtful? Would you assume she was "only teasing"?

She laughs, then says, "Just kidding."

Does this change your opinion of what Alice said to Stephanie? Does it cancel out any hurtfulness or negativity? Does it change your opinion of Alice herself or her friendship with Stephanie?

But despite that, Stephanie feels hurt. Alice gets annoyed; after all, she was only teasing. "What's wrong with you, Stephanie?" Alice retorts. "Can't you take a joke?" Alice turns to her other friends for support and they band together to defend Alice. "You're so sensitive, Stephanie! Alice was just teasing; she didn't mean anything by it!"

Who do you think is acting most maturely and responsibly in this story? Do you feel that Alice is wrong for teasing Stephanie? Do you feel that Stephanie is wrong for being too thin-skinned? Take a moment to think about these questions. Gather your own thoughts and feelings about teasing and about this story, then read on to hear our take on it.

Strip away all the scripts of what society calls acceptable and look behind that to see what's actually going on: teasing allows us to say hurtful things to someone without social consequences. We choose to communicate honesty and authentically, and teasing is neither.

Alice said mean things to Stephanie, but then "took them back" by saying that she was "just teasing." This way, Alice can verbally attack Stephanie without being accountable for her words. Teasing is a social "get out of trouble free card" that allows the teaser to say anything at all and to take zero responsibility for it.

Alice's intent does matter (she may have intended only humor and not offense) but the end result matters too. If Stephanie feels hurt as a result of Alice's unkind words, then "I didn't mean it" might not make Stephanie feel better. Words, once spoken, cannot be unspoken, and there are many ways to be funny without being hurtful.

Teasing is not nice, considerate, or positive. The dictionary defines teasing as "to vex, to annoy, to ridicule someone," and that's what you're doing when you tease. It may seem funny to you, but you may be making the usual error. You may have a thick skin, but that doesn't mean everyone else does.

If you're a parent, you've likely had to deal with your child coming to you after an incident in which they were the object of teasing; kids treat each other cruelly and adults allow this negative behavior because it's "just teasing." We're taught from a young age that we can say the nastiest things if we tack on "I'm just teasing!" to the end of whatever we say.

Not only is teasing a socially acceptable way to be mean, it's also a way to say anything you want with no fear of repercussion. "I was *teasing!*" gets you out of responsibility for the hurt you've caused someone else. Not only that, but teasing actually turns your victim into the villain, as in the story when Alice's friends blamed Stephanie for being too sensitive to "take a joke."

Another form of teasing, while more gentle, is hurtful in a different way: teasing can be limiting. We've already talked about rephrasing words that limit yourself; now we'll talk about ways in which words can limit *others*.

Kyeli's Story:

"Pace is Amusingly Unobservant!"[1]

Pace used to be very unobservant. She wouldn't see much going on around her and it often took a lot to get her to notice things. I would occasionally tease her about it by saying things like, "Even Pace would notice that!" when something was blatantly obvious. I always smiled and used a gentle tone, and she knew I meant no malice. For a long time, she was fine with it.

When we started focusing on the ill effects of teasing, we realized that even this gentle, playful form of teasing was harmful — I was limiting Pace by putting her in the *unobservant* box, both in my mind and in hers, by verbally reinforcing this nega-

---

1   This is the same story we told in Chapter 32: Rephrasing things positively, this time told from Kyeli's perspective instead of Pace's.

tive behavior. One afternoon, she announced that she was no longer unobservant and was going to pay attention to the world around her. I supported her by weeding out my teasing language and she became quite observant. Our relationship improved, too, because we felt closer to each other. I no longer teased her and she became more attentive!

As with "I'm only teasing," there are other socially acceptable phrases used to hurt others and get away with it. In the southern United States, one of these phrases is "Bless her heart." For example, a girl arrives late to a meeting. As the meeting disperses, one of the other people in attendance leans over and says in a sugary voice, "You just don't have the brains God gave a donkey, bless your heart. Can't tell time to save your soul." You can say the nastiest things, but as long as you append "bless her heart," it's completely socially acceptable.

"I'm just saying" is another poison dart. You can make any sort of inflammatory or insulting comment, but as long as you repeatedly say, "I'm just saying," it is difficult to socially justify calling you on your rudeness or meanness. "I'm just saying" is often accompanied by a defensive gesture of palms facing outward, nonverbally reinforcing the message of "Don't blame me! I said something, but I *just* said it, so that means I don't have to take any responsibility for it!" Being socially acceptable doesn't make it right or good to verbally hurt others. This is why we dislike teasing. It's hurtful, unhelpful, and disingenuous.

Teasing often functions as a defense mechanism, instinctively shot out to protect ourselves from what we feel is an attack, especially when we're in groups of our peers. We tend towards teasing when we feel threatened or upset, but don't want to let our true feelings show. Teasing can also be a cover for our feelings if we're afraid to be authentic or to ask for what we actually want: "If you miss my party, I will destroy you!" can be a teasing cover for "It hurt my feelings the last time you didn't come to my party, so please come this time."

Kyeli's Story: Teasing to Hide the Hurt

One evening, Pace decided at the last minute to stay home instead of go to a party with me as we'd previously planned. I went upstairs to get ready to go, and as I came back downstairs, she said she would miss me. I retorted, "I'll be having too much fun to miss *you*." She looked upset and said that I'd hurt her feelings. My initial reaction? "Oh! But I was *just teasing!*"

We talked it out. I realized I was upset because we'd been planning to go together for several weeks, and having her bail at the last minute hurt my feelings and even made me feel like she didn't want to be with me. She reassured me that wasn't the case, that she felt tired and antisocial, and she loved me and would, indeed, miss me. I apologized for teasing her and for hurting her feelings, she apologized for hurting mine, and I went on to the party in a much better mood.

Imagine how much better communication would be if we replaced teasing with open, honest, and authentic communication. Instead of "What's the matter? Can't read your digital watch?" rephrase to: "I'm feeling frustrated because we didn't start on time, and I would like some reassurance that you value our time together." Instead of "You look like a bird nested in your hair!" rephrase to: "Oh, did you notice that your hair looks a bit tangled today? Are you cool with that? If not, I'll be happy to help you brush it out." Instead of "Whoa, did you get dressed in the dark?" rephrase to: "Those colors don't look like they match to me. Do they look good to you?"

We can always express our feelings clearly and honestly, without hurting the recipient, if we give it some thought and consider the feelings of our partner. The next time you encounter teasing (as the teaser or the teasee) take a moment to think about the true message buried underneath the teasing. Wouldn't it be better to drop the teasing and simply communicate the underlying message itself?

CHAPTER 34:
ENDINGS

What if we told you that there is a simple, extremely effective way to make your days better, your relationships smoother, and unpleasant experiences more bearable? What if we said it doesn't require any willpower or study and very little practice? Wouldn't that be a great way to end the book?

Have you ever watched a movie or read a book, enjoyed the beginning, enjoyed the middle, and then had the entire experience ruined by an absolutely awful ending? What about the reverse: a mediocre reading or viewing experience redeemed by the way it all turned out in the end?

Endings have power, and not just in media. Imagine this: You're having a particularly awful day. Your car breaks down, it's raining, you get splashed by an inconsiderate passing car, there's a terrible mix-up at your job causing all sorts of stress, and you come home exhausted and unhappy. Later that night, you receive a long massage, your favorite dinner, and flowers from your partner. How would you look back upon that day as a whole?

We suggest you'd probably look back on it as a pretty good day and that your view would *certainly* be many times better than it would have been otherwise. How would it have been different if the pampering had come first instead of last?

The psychological power of endings has been proven scientifically. Take colonoscopy patients, for example.[1] A colonoscopy is not a comfortable procedure, but patients experience less discomfort when the probe is stationary. A control group underwent a normal colonoscopy and the experimental group had an extra special bit at the end where the probe was held stationary for an additional 60 seconds. The experimental group reported significantly more happiness with the procedure than the control group did. They also reported that they would be more willing to undergo another colonoscopy in the future.

Why? Because of the power of endings. Even though the people in the experimental group spent *more* total time with the uncomfortable probe inside them, the relatively minor discomfort of the final 60 seconds completely dominated their feelings and their memories of the procedure.

Kyeli's Story:

Wii Tennis Makes Everything Better

I was having a bad day. I had a bad dream and woke up scared, and it took me a long time to shake it off. I hurt my foot during my morning exercises. I ran out of shampoo in the shower, got cold trying to get a new bottle, and banged my elbow on the counter in the process. I forgot to eat breakfast and by lunch was so hungry I couldn't decide what to eat. I made a poor choice and wound up not enjoying my meal as well as getting indigestion afterward. I forgot an

---

1   We read about this study in some random article on the internet, but that article was based on this psychological study: "When More Pain Is Preferred to Less: Adding a Better End" by Kahneman, Fredrickson, Schreiber, and Redelmeier, published in 1993 in Psychological Science (Cambridge) volume 4, number 6, pages 401-405.

important work email and annoyed a client. I had an employee bail on a project and had to handle another annoyed client. Pace was feeling stressed, and she and I wound up arguing. I made dinner and wound up burning it.

But then, Pace ordered us pizza for dinner. She, Dru, and I watched an episode of one of my favorite shows. We cuddled on the couch. We played several rounds of Wii Tennis (the best video game ever!). We went to bed together and snuggled before sleep.

Just before I drifted off, my mind reviewed the day. All in all, I decided, not a bad day.

The next morning, I reflected on this. Not a bad day?! It had been so horrible! But it had *ended* extremely well; my favorite activities with my favorite people for just a few hours at the end of the day totally turned around my *entire day*.

It's an observable though often overlooked fact that our perceptions of enjoyment and unhappiness are influenced far more by what happens at the end of something than by what happens at the beginning or somewhere in the middle. If something ends well, we tend to look upon it favorably. If something ends badly, we look upon it unfavorably.

Kyeli's Story: *Escaflowne*

A year or so ago, we watched *Escaflowne,* an anime series. This started out as the greatest anime I'd ever seen! It had fantasy, sci-fi, typical anime stuff, weird and interesting plot, love stories, giant battle mechs; just about anything a fan could want out of an anime series.

Then came the last episode.

In the last episode, the main character made a decision that blew me away. It was against everything the entire 26-episode series had been working up to and left me completely frustrated. As a result, I felt cheated and upset. I just spent some 14 hours of my life watching this horrible series!

Never mind that the previous 25 episodes had been *awesome,* that the story to that point was incredible — that one episode, the ending, ruined the entire series for me!

Guess what? Knowing this gives you power. Through simple scheduling, you can now make any potentially unpleasant thing more bearable. Simply make sure to schedule fun or relaxing things directly after the dreaded event. Put your less fun tasks closer to the beginning of your day, rather than near the end. If something emotionally difficult comes up with your partner in the evening, make sure to get some relaxing, cuddling, or other such happy bonding time after, so as to not end on a sour note.

Even if you don't schedule the happy things at the end, or even if you tried to and it didn't work out, being aware of the power of endings can improve your life. If something bad or stressful happens near the end of your day, your conversation, your vacation, or whatever, remind yourself of the power of endings. Remember when you look back, it wasn't *really* as bad as you think it was; you're magnifying the badness because of this ending bias. Take a little time to review the good things that happened earlier and put things into a perspective where the bad thing that happened at the end was one bad thing among several good things. See?

It's that simple. It's helped our lives enormously, and it can help you, too!

STORIES AND EXAMPLES

Kyeli's Story: Making the Usual Error . . . . p. 6

Joan and Larry's Example:
        The Flaw in the Golden Rule . . . . p. 8

Kyeli's Story: Differences in Our Household . . . . p. 11

Kyeli's Story: "I'm Not Yelling!" . . . . p. 12

Pace's Story: "I'm Really Okay" . . . . p. 13

Pace's Story: It Might Be Nice
        to See a Movie on Sunday . . . . p. 15

Pace's Story: Cardboard Cutout Keith . . . . p. 18

Walter's Example: A Conversation with Yohn . . . . p. 19

Kyeli's Story: Falling in Love . . . . p. 20

Kevin's Example: Triad Check-In Time . . . . p. 24

Kyeli's Story: Blammo! . . . . p. 30

Pace's Story: Don Needs a Widget . . . . p. 32

Steve's Example: Fred Needs Quality Time . . . . p. 33

Kyeli's Story: What Are We Doing? . . . . p. 34

Kyeli's Story: The Road Trip . . . . p. 36

Rebeka's Example: Music vs. Video . . . . p. 38

Becky's Example: Too Late for the Show . . . . p. 42

Kyeli's Story: Rate Your Cleanliness
        on a Scale from 1 to 10 . . . . p. 45

Stories and Examples

Gryphon's Story: The Clawless
Swipe of Fierceness . . . . p. 48

Kyeli's Story: Improv Night . . . . p. 49

Kyeli's Story: Let's Talk About Text, Baby! . . . . p. 54

Kyeli's Story: Buy Me a Present! . . . . p. 55

Kyeli's Story: Drawing Down the Lightning . . . . p. 58

Kyeli's Story: In My Perspective . . . . p. 62

Kyeli's Story: The Urgent Email . . . . p. 67

Pace's Story: Kyeli's Kidney Stone . . . . p. 68

Michelle and Anthony's Example:
It's All About Me . . . . p. 69

Michelle and Anthony's Example:
It's Not All About Me . . . . p. 70

Kyeli's Story: Pace Humiliates
Me in Front of Our Friends . . . . p. 77

Kyeli's Story: The Best Veggie Burger Ever! . . . . p. 80

Kyeli's Story: Care and
Feeding of the Wild Pace . . . . p. 82

Kyeli's Story: Defuse Me Like a Bomb . . . . p. 84

Pace's Story: Design vs. Design — Fight! . . . . p. 86

Mary and Kathi's Example: A Few Sandwiches . . . . p. 88

Kyeli's Story: Define Your Date . . . . p. 91

Pace's Story: Learning to Emote . . . . p. 96

Pace's Story: Meta-Money . . . . p. 96

Kyeli's Story: A Tangent of Reconnection . . . . p. 97

Stories and Examples

Kyeli's Story: A Bear at the Door . . . . p. 100

Kyeli's Story: Tom and Flat Cat . . . . p. 102

Pace's Story: Trusting My Future Self . . . . p. 106

Kyeli's Story: It's My Party,
    and I'll Go If I Want To! . . . . p. 107

Pace's Story: Playing Video Games . . . . p. 110

Kyeli's Story: Scream Real Loud! . . . . p. 115

Kyeli's Story: Richard's Email Stew . . . . p. 116

Jane and Joe's Example:
    Shattering the Stereotype . . . . p. 119

Kyeli's Story: In the Zone . . . . p. 121

Claire's Example: A Baseline . . . . p. 124

Claire's Example: Dropped! . . . . p. 125

Claire's Example: Bonus! . . . . p. 125

Kyeli's Story: Motivation and Money . . . . p. 128

Pace's Story: Missed Connection . . . . p. 130

Pace's Story: Privacy vs. Secrecy . . . . p. 133

Allison & Billy and Corey & Donovan's Example:
    Religion vs. Polka . . . . p. 136

Kyeli's Story: Being Right About Nalia . . . . p. 137

Kyeli's Story: Why Am I Doing This? . . . . p. 140

Kyeli's Story: Not Enough Blue! . . . . p. 149

Kyeli's Story: It's Super Effective! . . . . p. 151

Kyeli's Story: Happiness Squared . . . . p. 155

Pace's Story: Pace Needs More Alone Time . . . . p. 158

Stories and Examples

Pace's Story: Pace Needs More Alone Time (Reprise) . . . . p. 159

Kyeli's Story: The Oubliette . . . . p. 163

Kyeli's Story: The Piano Myth . . . . p. 169

Pace's Story: "I'm Not Very Observant" . . . . p. 172

Stephanie's Example: Don't Tease My Hair! . . . . p. 175

Kyeli's Story: "Pace Is Amusingly Unobservant!" . . . . p. 177

Kyeli's Story: Teasing to Hide the Hurt . . . . p. 179

Kyeli's Story: Wii Tennis Makes Everything Better . . . . p. 182

Kyeli's Story: Escaflowne . . . . p. 183

Illustrations

p. 4

p. 10

p. 14

p. 17

p. 22

p. 28

p. 32

pp. 36, 39

p. 42

Illustrations

p. 44

p. 47

pp. 52, 53

p. 57

pp. 61, 65

p. 66

p. 74

p. 79

pp. 84, 87

p. 88

p. 95

p. 99

p. 105

p. 108

p. 114

p. 118

pp. 124–126

p. 132

Illustrations

p. 139

pp. 143-147

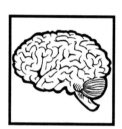

p. 154

p. 157

pp. 161, 162

p. 165

p. 174

p. 185

About the Authors

Pace studied logic and computer science at Carnegie Mellon University and worked in the field of artificial intelligence for about a decade. In 2005, she had a life-changing spiritual experience and realized that her true calling lay elsewhere. Since then, she has been following her passion and deepening her connections with herself and others. She loves to learn about communication and many other exciting things, and she loves to share what she's learned.

Kyeli started on this path of communication in 2004, when she broke out of a lifelong haze. She jumped into a vast world of rapid self- and relationship work, and began getting messy and making mistakes right off the bat, with passion, strength, and joy previously unknown to herself. She discovered her spiritual path, fell in love with herself, and began cultivating a chosen community full of awesome people.

Pace and Kyeli live in Austin, Texas with their son Dru and far too many cats. They love to talk, so if you have questions or comments, email them: **pace@usualerror.com** and **kyeli@usualerror.com**.

About the Illustrator

Martin Whitmore graduated from Youngstown State University with a BFA in Art & Technology in 2004. Shortly thereafter he left a trail of broken hearts and buried bodies on his way to Austin, Texas to pursue a career as an illustrator. He found an outlet for his unhealthy obsession with zombies and pinup girls in his webcomic, Tasty Flesh, at **www.tastyflesh.com**.

You can find out about Marty's latest projects, events, and insane rantings on his website (**www.martinwhitmore.com**), or you can contact him directly at **marty@martinwhitmore.com**.

About the Usual Error Project

If you'd like to see a Usual Error workshop in your city, email us at **workshops@usualerror.com**. For more information on authentic communication, including this entire book in text and PDF form, visit our website: **www.usualerror.com**. This book is just the tip of the Usual Error iceberg!

Printed in the United Kingdom by
Lightning Source UK Ltd., Milton Keynes
138305UK00001B/48/P